SET FOR LIFE

SET FOR LIFE

USE PROPERTY TO BUILD WEALTH, CREATE FREEDOM AND LEAVE A LEGACY

LLOYD EDGE

WILEY

First published 2026 by John Wiley & Sons Australia, Ltd

ISBN: 978-1-394-43478-7

A catalogue record for this book is available from the National Library of Australia

Registered Office
John Wiley & Sons Australia, Ltd. Level 4, 600 Bourke Street, Melbourne, VIC 3000, Australia

For details of our global editorial offices, customer services, and more information about Wiley products visit us at www.wiley.com.

Wiley also publishes its books in a variety of electronic formats and by print-on-demand. Some content that appears in standard print versions of this book may not be available in other formats.

Cover design by Wiley
Cover Image: © Nizwa Design/Adobe Stock

Author Photo: Sophie Brown

Set in 11/16 pts and Palatino LT Std by Straive, Chennai, India.

To Renee, my lifelong partner.
One life, one love—set for life.

Contents

About the author

Lloyd Edge has more than 20 years' experience in the property market. He is the founder and CEO of Aus Property Professionals, one of Australia's leading buyers' agencies, with a team across multiple states in Australia. He is also a celebrated property investor and author of the bestselling books *Positively Geared* and *Buy Now*. He began his work life on a very different track, as a music teacher and conductor, before transitioning to property investment. Starting out with a $30 000 deposit, he built a formidable property portfolio that is now worth more than $30 million, including his multimillion-dollar Sydney waterfront home and his holiday home at Mollymook.

Lloyd soon replaced his earned income with passive income from property investments, which allowed him to retire from the 'rat race' at 40.

In 2024 the REINSW Awards for Excellence named him Buyers' Agent of the Year; he was also a finalist in *CEO Magazine*'s Executive of the Year Awards in both 2024 and 2025. He has received several Real Estate Business (REB) Awards; and in 2022 Aus Property Professionals won Property Investment Strategist of the Year in the Australian Enterprise Awards.

Lloyd's expertise and strategies have made him a household name. He regularly contributes on major media outlets and hosts the popular *Positively Geared* podcast. Lloyd has leveraged his teaching background and firsthand experience into demystifying property investment and guiding others towards financial freedom. By doing so he hopes to empower Australians, no matter what their starting point or time frame, to attain their financial, lifestyle and legacy goals.

These days Lloyd can often be seen on TV commenting on the property markets. He has appeared on Channels 7, 9 and 10, Sky News and SBS. He has been interviewed on top-rated radio stations 2GB, 3AW and 6PR multiple times, and he currently has a regular column in *Australian Property Investor* magazine. Lloyd is on 'speed dial' with several journalists and is always happy to provide comment on relevant property stories.

Lloyd is proud to be able to give back in increasingly significant ways through Aus Property Professionals. He donates to a number of charitable organisations in Australia and abroad.

Above all he loves spending time with his family, whether out on the boat fishing, swimming or riding jet skis, or at martial arts sessions.

Acknowledgements

I never thought I'd publish again so soon after *Positively Geared*, 2nd edition, was released in early 2025. When the good folk at Wiley approached me to ask if I'd write another book, I knew the task would be mammoth, but I also knew we were up for it. I say 'we', as this one is a team effort with my fantastic developmental editorial team, who took on the challenge with me and kept me on track.

A massive thank you and much appreciation to Anna Warwick, who again worked very closely with me on this book. It was a massive task to prepare this one to the standard I wanted in the time we had between conception and delivery.

Alongside Anna have been our sub-editors, Merran White and Rowan Crosby, who were also up for the challenge. Many thanks for your contribution.

I would also like to thank the team at Wiley, who have always had confidence in me to produce books to the standard they require.

Thank you very much to my wife, Renee, who supports all my endeavours. This book is part of my legacy for our kids, and I look forward to their reading it when they are a little older.

Thanks to our team at Aus Property Professionals, which continues to grow. What started as a relatively modest venture for me as a sole trader has exploded into a company with many staff and multiple locations across the country.

I value our many clients who trust us to build their property portfolios and wealth. It's a task we take very seriously and take great pride in.

Finally, my thanks to you, my readers, for picking up *Set for Life*. I hope it inspires you on your own journey.

This book is for educational purposes only. The author and the publisher make no guarantees regarding results and disclaim liability for any damages or losses incurred from the use of the advice herein. Your own results may vary from the case studies you read in this book. Always obtain your own legal advice before signing any property contract.

At the time of writing, changes to negative gearing and the capital gains tax discount have been proposed by the Australian Government. Please check with your accountant/advisor to confirm if these changes impact you.

Introduction

How can you set yourself up financially for life right now? First you need to figure out exactly where you are today and where you want to be. You can then work back from there, planning the best step-by-step strategy for you to generate wealth through property.

And it's never too late to start.

Wherever you are in your life's journey, this book will guide you toward having some savings and some passive income coming in so you're not just relying on a pension when you retire. You feel empowered to rise above the naysayers and doom-and-gloomers, no matter how well-meaning they are, so you're never derailed on your property search again.

It's not about owning 10 or 20 or 30 or 50 properties. It's about setting yourself up with *enough*, so you can spend more time on things like your health, your passions, your favourite people—more time on *living*.

You'll hear me use the term 'freedom fund' a lot in this book, so let's define it properly from the start. Your freedom fund starts with those first few bucks you squirrel away in a savings account, separate from your everyday account, first as a buffer against life's unplanned adventures, then to use for your planned adventures. And over time it grows and grows.

As you keep saving, and maybe earn more income, your freedom fund grows into a deposit for your first property…and that's the last deposit you will ever need to save. Easy, right?

In the first three chapters of this book I'll tell you how to overcome savings challenges and start saving. Perhaps, like me, you are a frugal budgeter with a freedom fund just itching to be invested. In chapter 4 I'll show you some tried and tested strategies, and how to tailor them to your starting points and goals, so your freedom fund grows and grows.

A fully grown freedom fund combines savings, investments and income-producing assets and allows you to live comfortably without relying entirely on your job, business or, eventually, the age pension. It gives you options.

It doesn't mean you necessarily stop working; it does mean you have the freedom to choose. Many people with freedom funds continue to work—because they enjoy it. The point is they don't *have* to.

Getting to that point is what this book is all about. With a freedom fund you're essentially *set for life*.

The book is organised in such a way that no matter where you are in life, you'll be able to find strategies to help you realise *your* current financial goals. The first chapters will help you clarify what those goals are, at the heart of what's truly important to you in life—that is, the non-negotiables.

When you have a really firm grasp of what your goals are, I'll show you how to get your strategy together. Property is my preferred form of investment, but to purchase real estate you first need to have your personal finances in order. You need to be prepared to buy. That's in chapter 4.

I'll show you how to build that freedom fund regardless of your circumstances. If you're in your twenties, I'll show you how to invest your way to an early retirement. If you're in your thirties, I'll outline how you can expand your portfolio using different strategies to pay off your mortgage or build an asset base.

If you are in your forties or fifties, you'll probably have more assets. There are ways you can leverage what you already have and build quickly to set yourself up for an early retirement. If you are in your sixties you may be asset-rich but cash-poor. I can help get you set up for a comfortable retirement right now.

Whether you're young and near the bottom of the career ladder, or middle-aged and in a senior role at work while caring for others at home, or retiring, downsizing and ready to relax, this book will show you how to create your dream life through property investing.

At its heart, *Set for Life* is about creating a legacy, be that generational wealth for your kids and grandkids or giving back to a charity and the community, or both.

If I can do it, so can you.

This is my third book. My first, *Positively Geared (PG)*, focused on investment strategies. I shared the story of how this country kid progressed from high-school music teacher to financially independent property investor with enough passive income to retire from teaching at age 40.

My second book, *Buy Now*, laid out how to buy a dream home for yourself. I talked about the strategies I used to create my property portfolio so Renee and I could buy and pay off our own dream home; and about how I secured the best properties for myself and for my clients as a buyer's agent.

In this book I'll help you take care of business for yourself, your loved ones and the next generation through property investment. But you need to be willing to learn and to grow.

If you're financially overwhelmed and time-poor and want to take back control of your financial life, this book is for you. It's not just about the typical strategies: building a duplex, making a fantastic amount of money. That's the focus of my other books. This book is about what you can do to make a real, substantial difference in your life, given your current situation, even if it requires a huge mindshift.

You'll find plenty of property experts out there talking about how rich their clients are and how many properties their clients own. My buyer's agency, Aus Property Professionals, can make that boast too, but for us it's also about helping people extricate themselves from the messy life and financial situations they are in.

Many of my clients seek advice on getting out of a financial hole, and that's one thing I definitely can help you with. I'll discuss all sorts of successful strategies and illustrate them through case studies from my clients. I'll also explain how I dug myself out of my own hole.

A lot of people now come to me for help, because once they've read my books they feel they can relate to and trust me. My story resonates with them. They say, 'I feel like I know you already.' From the first phone call they're already talking about how I grew up in Orange or how I bought my first property in Rockdale.

In *Positively Geared* I talked about how it took me 10 years to replace my teacher's income at the time ($100 000) with $100 000 in passive income. I talked about building up my portfolio, studying for my real-estate licence, becoming a buyer's agent and getting the business going.

Now, 23 years later, at age 51, I can call myself an expert. I've been going through the property investment process with clients from start to finish, week in and week out, for over a decade. I've built an 18-property portfolio and helped thousands of Aussies buy more than $2.5 billion worth of property. In my second book, *Buy Now,* I discuss my entire portfolio and how I got there, step by step.

These days my passive income through property is a lot higher, and the business has grown, so I have different streams of cash flow coming through.

As an investor, I'm still in the acquisition phase but I've also been selling properties, and paying off properties in my portfolio. Our dream home in Sydney is fully paid off now, as is our holiday home on the coast. I've paid off other assets too.

We do still have assets with some debt, but they're generating cash flow, and the debt is part of various tax strategies we're employing. With every one of those assets there's a plan for how long we'll keep it and how we'll pay it off.

We've got money in the bank too.

I think it's important to talk about how I set myself up, but also to acknowledge that where I am in life today isn't where a lot of readers are at this point. What I've built isn't necessarily what *you* want. And this book is designed for you.

You might say it isn't really about buying property per se, as my other books are. It's about property as a strategy for gaining financial freedom, about how to get that end result.

Chapter 1

How to build your freedom fund

One of the biggest misconceptions I see in relation to personal finance, especially in Australia, is that owning your home outright automatically means you're financially secure. On paper, that might be true. In reality, it often isn't.

This chapter unravels the difference between being asset-rich and being cash-flow secure. They're not the same thing. You can own a multimillion-dollar home and still struggle with everyday expenses.

I meet people like this all the time—retirees whose houses in great suburbs are fully paid off yet who rely heavily on their pension and worry about unexpected costs.

That situation is largely the result of how most of us were taught to think about money. Work hard, buy your home, pay it off and 'everything will take care of itself' in retirement. For previous generations that strategy sometimes worked. Today it often leaves people asset-rich but income-poor.

This is why I talk so much about building a *freedom fund*. It's not just about owning assets. It's about owning assets that generate income, flexibility and peace of mind.

If you retire and must rely on the pension, you're depending on the government to support you. To avoid this you need cash flow. You need assets to pay you a salary. That's why investing matters.

It's not just about buying property. You might choose to invest in shares or gold or oil—in all sorts of things. You need some assets that will generate cash flow to enable you to retire when you want to and live comfortably.

You don't want to get to the end of your career and think, we've got a few years left—let's enjoy it on the pension! You want to set yourself up well and retire early so you can enjoy life to the full. I'm here to help you do that. I love helping other Aussies *invest smart* so they can live comfortably and create a positive legacy. Truly, it's what gets me out of bed every day.

This book is not about being a multi-millionaire with a big portfolio of properties or owning that massive house. It's about working toward being comfortable for life.

In this chapter, we're going to unpack why so many Australians work hard but end up with no freedom fund because what looks like wealth on paper—owning a multimillion-dollar house, say—doesn't translate into financial freedom. This chapter is about what you can do differently.

Set your goal

Most buyer's agents will focus on advising you on buying a property. The first thing I do with a new client isn't to look at property; it's to ask, 'Where are you in your life? What are you trying to achieve? Let's map out a plan, a strategy, and then think about property. The first thing I want you to consider is your current financial situation. Do you have a freedom fund?'

People seek financial advice as they reach different life stages. It really comes down to goal-setting, resolving what you're trying to achieve and working backwards from there.

It's a big-picture perspective.

A new client may say something like, 'I'm 45 and I don't have much saved, but I want to be in a better position by 55. So I want to start a property portfolio.' Maybe they've gone through a divorce, or their business has gone under or they've lost their job.

A lot of my clients are single and starting to climb the career ladder. They may be in their early twenties but already seeing the writing on the wall if they choose to take the path their parents followed. They may fear they will never own a home given the current markets.

There are single parents with young kids and couples with young kids and elderly parents. There are single women and widows who need a home. And there are your regular families with two-and-a-half kids and a dog.

All of which is to say, there's everybody! I can speak to every reader because I've worked with all sorts of people in my 12-plus years of running the business. And every single situation is different.

People's goals may be similar, but none are the same. I talk with hundreds of people each week and all their stories are different. Some have no money; some have lots. Some earn a lot but have zero savings. Some have property that hasn't done very well for them; others may have a productive portfolio.

They may have adult kids or grandkids, and want to set themselves up financially in order to help the kids. Some come to me in their fifties and ask, 'How can I buy my dream home on the water in the next 10 years.' Realistically, that's not going to happen unless they have some savings and somewhere to start. It won't happen by magic.

Some people might already have their dream home paid off but have no cash and want to set up a passive income.

I have plenty of clients who have lost a parent and inherited some money and want help investing that money to set themselves up.

I've worked with so many people whose first question is, 'Have we left it too late?' And my answer is always a firm 'No'. However, I do advise my retirement-age clients to seek financial advice by speaking with a financial planner. We can all sit in on that conversation and have a round-table discussion.

There's a solution for just about every challenging situation. It comes down to what's important to you and what you are trying to achieve. But you don't have to take my word for it. In this book, we'll look at many success stories from clients who were in situations just like those I've enumerated and the property investment strategies that helped them get ahead.

Case study

From divorce to financial independence

Katie, in her mid-fifties, came to me having read the first edition of *Positively Geared*. She was single, had spent many years out of the workforce raising kids and had only $90 000 in super — nowhere near enough to retire on.

Recently divorced, she was in a difficult position financially. She'd gone from a double-income family to living alone on a single income, as her children were no longer dependants.

As part of the divorce, she kept the investment properties — an apartment in inner Brisbane and a townhouse in Adelaide — but because they were negatively geared, the rents weren't covering the mortgage and she was having trouble keeping up with them as well her own rent.

What she wanted

Katie wanted to set herself up for retirement, but on a single income and with little super she needed sound financial advice.

In our discovery call I ran through a few scenarios. She wasn't comfortable renting at her age, and the aim was to get her in a position to buy her forever home. Katie's dream was to move to the Gold Coast.

To achieve this goal, she needed to build her cash flow and acquire some properties that would both help offset the low cash flow on her existing properties and build her freedom fund.

The strategy

I suggested that because Katie's Adelaide asset wasn't performing well, she should sell it to reduce her debt and improve her position with the banks. I urged her to go back to her broker to run some numbers and get a pre-approval.

Katie had $90 000 in cash for a deposit on another investment property, and her broker prepared a pre-approval for a loan of up to $625 000. Her total budget, including the deposit, was

(continued)

just over $700 000. The key was to spend less than that and maximise cash flow.

Property 1: Armidale, NSW

We sourced a very good property in Armidale, NSW, a city that was going through its next growth phase.

- *Purchase price:* $525 000 (well under Katie's budget)
- *Rental income:* $625 per week
- *Yield:* 6.1 per cent
- *Result:* rented immediately

Katie then sold her Adelaide townhouse for $650 000. This increased her total borrowing capacity to $1.1 million for her next purchase.

Property 2: Deception Bay, Brisbane

I could see that market growth in Brisbane was about to happen. We secured a fantastic four-bedroom house with two bathrooms, a double garage and a media room in the northern Brisbane suburb of Deception Bay for $725 000.

- *Purchase price:* $725 000
- *Rental income:* $650 per week
- *Yield:* 4.6 per cent (very good for the area where most yields are 4 per cent or under)
- *Secured:* off-market
- *18-month valuation:* $925 000
- *Equity gain:* $200 000 in just 18 months

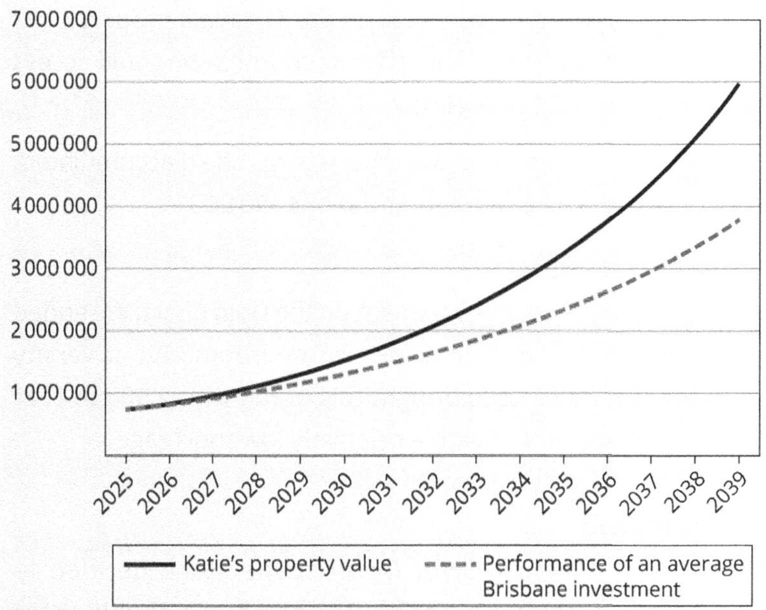

Figure 1.1 *Estimated property value over time*

Watching the growth

Katie sat on these properties and watched their growth with excitement. We kept her up-to-date with what the market was doing.

Eighteen months later the market started to boom. With retirement approaching, we decided it was time to sell down the Armidale property to finance her forever home.

The sale strategy

Armidale sold for $710 000 — a $185 000 profit in 18 months. Deception Bay was valued at $925 000 — a $200 000 increase in 18 months.

(continued)

Katie had to pay capital gains tax on the Armidale property, but because she'd held it for more than 12 months she could access the 50 per cent CGT reduction.

After taxes, and combined with the savings she'd accumulated, Katie now had a freedom fund total of $450 000.

The forever home

Her dream home was an apartment on the Gold Coast. We ended up acquiring a low-maintenance two-bedroom unit at Varsity Lakes for $855 000. Katie bought this home with a 50 per cent deposit, leaving herself with a relatively low mortgage.

The outcome

Given the predicted growth for Brisbane, Katie decided to keep her property in Deception Bay and buy a couple more properties with my help. Katie's goal is to pay down her Varsity Lakes home as soon as possible, to set herself up for life. She has graduated from struggling on a single income to financial security in retirement.

Katie's freedom fund strategy

- Challenge: Divorced, single income, negatively geared properties.
- Strategy: Sell underperforming assets, buy high-yield properties, sell at a profit.
- Property 1 (Armidale): $525 000 to $710 000 = $185 000 profit. CGT benefit: 50 per cent reduction for holding over 12 months.

- Property 2 (Deception Bay): $725 000 to $925 000 = $200 000 profit + $200 000 equity in 18 months. Property is positively geared.
- Forever home: $855 000 apartment with 50% deposit (low mortgage).
- Note here that age didn't matter. With the right strategy, starting over at age 50+ still works.

Next phase: Keep one investment, buy more to pay down the forever home faster and start enjoying a passive income from a positively geared portfolio.

NET YIELD is the income on an investment after costs and expenses, including purchasing and transaction costs such as stamp duty, legal fees, pest and building inspections, loan start-up fees, advertising, rent lost through vacancy, repairs and maintenance, management fees, insurance, rates and charges.

Tap into the reasons why

For me, money means peace of mind. Now, if something happens—an emergency with the kids or the car or the dog—I know we'll be okay. It's about knowing my family is taken care of today and I won't be a burden tomorrow. In fact, I hope I will have made life much easier for them through creating a legacy of generational wealth.

It means I will have built a life I love to live. It's really about freedom. A lot of people post fancy shots of their cars and their boat and all the cool things they do on Instagram. I've always loved cars, but I don't think I've ever put up anything online about my cars.

The first car I ever had was a secondhand Mini I bought from a friend of my dad's. It was a 1972 model and I bought it in 1992, during my final year of school. The next car was a secondhand Ford Falcon that had been a taxi and had about 500 000 kilometres on the clock.

I had achieved financial independence and left teaching before I bought my first 'cool' car—a Mercedes convertible. Recently I bought my dream car, but that's because I put myself in a position to be able to do that.

It's great if you can afford nice cars and things but when it comes down to it, it's about buying comfort, leisure and, most important, time, because the most important things in life are having time to spend with your family and friends. To borrow a cliché, you only live once. To enjoy those precious times, you need a freedom fund more than you need a fancy car.

What makes your perfect day?

If you're having trouble visualising a life goal, here's a quick way to figure out what you want.

Ask yourself, If I had one day to live and I could do anything at all in that day, what would I do?

We live on the water now, opposite a national park. The perfect day for me involves taking the kids to the beach. Spending time together on the boat. The day Riley caught his first fish was just amazing. We take lunch with us and just have a nice day out on the water. That's my perfect day.

Riley's first catch

Work backwards from a passive income goal

Now you know what you truly want—that last-day-on-Earth scenario—you can look at your financial situation and ask: Do I have cash available for that? Am I broke, in debt? Am I still working? Can I get a loan? Where are the risks? What can I invest in? Can I go into partnership with someone else, maybe with one of my kids, to buy property to help us both get ahead?

Let me show you, in a nutshell, what I do with my clients each day to give them a bigger-picture view of their finances. We'll start with the goal: paying yourself an annual cash flow of, say, $100 000, so you have time for your perfect day, 365 days a year.

You'll need $150 000 a year in rent, because if you're aiming for something fairly achievable like $30 000 a year in rental income from each property, then you'll need about five properties to clear around $100 000 a year in actual income by the time you've paid all your expenses.

Of course, it's not going to be passive income until you have paid off any debt against them. To keep that amount, all those properties need to be unencumbered by mortgages.

So you need strategies in place, first to buy properties and then to pay them off. And property investment becomes trickier as you get older because you have less time to allow the properties to increase in value or to pay them off. In this situation, you'll need an 'exit plan'. For example, you might buy twice as many properties as you want to end up with, then sell half of them to pay off the other half.

There is a strategy for everyone.

Property as an asset

Australians love property. Owning our own slice of land is the Great Aussie Dream and part of our culture. It's also one of the country's most resilient and profitable investment vehicles. But buying property to become rich just doesn't work as it once did.

Why not? Because Australia isn't just one property market—it's thousands. Every suburb, every street can behave differently, based on supply, demand, interest rates and population growth. If you don't have a strategy that takes all this into account, you are not investing; you're guessing.

Not everyone needs to buy property. Some people's financial situation and goals mean it's better for them to focus on other asset classes. I chose property over other asset classes, such as stocks, when I began investing because that's what I was exposed to.

And I liked that the property market was less nebulous and less volatile than others. You can see, touch and feel property, and it takes longer to sell and longer to buy. That met my need for security.

Stocks can go up and down overnight. The share market can plummet over something a politician says or does, or over something that happens overseas. Property doesn't work that way, and because it takes longer to crash, or to rise, it's a bit safer.

Property as an investment strategy hasn't essentially changed since I began investing. In chapter 4 we look at how property has the ability to double your wealth in a short space of time. You can change your life quickly, which is exactly what I've done.

Some strategies will change from time to time depending on, for example, rising construction costs or decreasing rental yields. Today it's pretty hard to find positively geared properties that offer the trifecta—low interest rates, high rental yields and capital growth—compared to a few years ago, when interest rates were lower.

THE PROPERTY TRIFECTA

But maybe positively geared properties aren't as important as some people think. And as an investment, I believe property is as good today as it was when I first invested.

Invest with a strategy: a roadmap to property success

If you're chasing financial freedom, it's not about luck. It's about having a strategy. Following are the strategies I'll cover here:

1. Capital growth

Let's start with the classic 'buy and hold'. You purchase in a well-located suburb with strong demand and you hold for the long term in order to benefit from rising values. This is perfect for wealth accumulation, retirement planning or building equity to grow your portfolio, but holding might cost you in the short term. Some high-growth properties are not positively geared, so you'll need to be able to cover the cash-flow gap caused by a low rental return.

2. Cash-flow strategy

Cash-flow investing is all about buying properties that generate high rental income. You might look in regional areas or lower-priced suburbs where yields are strong. It's great for building a passive income but often comes with less capital growth. So if long-term wealth is your goal, cash flow alone won't get you there. We'll talk about markets in chapter 6.

3. Manufacture equity

Equity is the difference between the market value of the property and what you owe on it.

If you don't want to wait for the market to move, you can increase a property's value by, say, renovating or by developing a dual-income property—think a granny flat or a duplex. Just be warned, reno blowouts, council delays and tight selling windows can turn quick profit into slow pain. We'll look at strategies later.

4. Positively geared portfolio

Positive gearing and balanced portfolios are a smart move. Blending strategies can create a balanced portfolio in which high-yield properties help cover the shortfalls from capital growth ones, enabling you to build a positively geared portfolio without sacrificing long-term wealth creation. I'll tell you about this in chapter 11.

5. Negative gearing

For high-income earners, negative gearing might be part of the plan. You wear short-term losses on paper, use them to reduce your taxable income and wait for capital growth to make up the difference. But this works only if you can afford the shortfall. It's not a strategy for investors who are just scraping by.

6. Self-managed super fund

You can invest through a self-managed super fund. This strategy gives you control of your retirement savings and offers tax advantages, such as tax-free rental income and capital gains once you reach the pension phase. You can also use borrowing structures inside an SMSF, but there are a lot of rules, so get advice and understand the restrictions before jumping in. I'll explain more in chapter 9.

7. Time frame

You need a time frame for your goal. If you're in your twenties, you might want to retire by the time you're 40. If you're in your thirties you might be seeking the freedom of another income stream or no mortgage so you can spend more time with your children while they're young.

If you're in your fifties, maybe you're trying to achieve $100 000 a year in passive income by the time you're 65. Some can do that in 10 years, depending on their income.

If you're 60, we're not talking about achieving $100 000 by age 65 unless you're planning to keep working. Lenders are less likely to look favourably on you because they know you're not likely to keep working and paying off a 30-year loan until you're 90. You'll want to retire!

That's where downsizing becomes important. Sell the home, buy something smaller and invest the difference, or buy an investment property outright and use the rent from that as passive income.

Case study

The clients

Let me introduce Michael and Melissa. Their goals were clear: retire early, build passive income and eventually fund their dream home using equity, not savings. Here's what we did.

The strategy

First, they bought a regional property (for $395 000) that was already renting at $450 a week. Six months later they spent just $22 000 on a smart cosmetic renovation — think paint, flooring, fixtures.

The result

A new valuation on their property of $550 000. The rent jumped to $490 a week and it's on track to hit $520. Their yield: close to 6.8 per cent. The property is now positively geared and they've tapped into the new equity to fund investment number two. They could do this because they had one thing most investors don't: a strategy tailored to their goals. This isn't about buying cheap or relying on luck. It's about executing the right move at the right time with the right plan.

Your right to live comfortably

It doesn't have to be stressful! My whole philosophy is about setting yourself up so you can live a comfortable, stress-free life. Whether you plan to retire at 65 or at 50, you'll have worked hard to get there and you want to be comfortable.

This is about you. Not everyone needs $100 000 in passive income a year. If you've paid off all your debt — you've got no car loans and no mortgages — $40 000 or $50 000 a year might be enough.

The key is to be comfortable. Sure, when we're young, many of us are trying to keep up with the Joneses: striving for the next house, the next car. But people who live like this risk getting into substantial debt. I get it. You deserve to enjoy what you've worked for.

Many people tell me they want a worry-free life. I prioritise helping them set themselves up so they can be comfortable and free of stress in their retirement years. So don't worry about 'keeping up' with others.

Just work out what you need for a happy and comfortable retirement and work toward making that a reality.

What are your inherited beliefs?

Maybe you're not keen on overextending yourself financially or taking on a long and complex property investment project. Maybe all this is new. I get it. I gave no thought to property as an investment until I was 28. I grew up on a farm about 10 kilometres out of Orange. My parents didn't invest in property and they were strict believers in paying cash for everything. Our farmhouse was a place to live rather than an investment opportunity.

Back then everything was orchards—not oranges, but apples. After hailstorms devastated the orchards some growers turned to winemaking. The region is now famous for wine—not apples or oranges.

My brother now owns and lives on the family farm our dad bought for about $20 000 in the 1970s. The last valuation, a couple of years ago, was about $2 million. That's compounding capital growth for you.

I became passionate about property when I recognised it as a vehicle for building wealth. It was clear to me my dad's philosophy of 'If you can't afford to pay cash for it, you shouldn't buy it' wouldn't enable me to follow my passion, because I would need to use debt to create wealth.

Buying an investment property needs bank financing. That's why property is so good as an investment. It's a great way to leverage money.

I'm the first person in my family to branch out and use leverage to create wealth. The point is, Dad did save the money he had, but he didn't make much.

A family man

I don't remember any financial hard times during my childhood. Dad was a business owner who never carried any debt, but we weren't wealthy.

I remember Dad working really long hours. He would come home from work at six or seven each night and work on the farm for a few hours. He'd be out there watering trees, fencing and stuff like that.

At the time it never bothered me. Mum was a nurse but once she had kids she stayed home with us. So I always had one parent around when I was younger, and both of them once Dad retired. They were always there. Even when he was still working he would often come home at lunchtime to spend time with Mum. He was always a family man.

When Dad retired in 1984 he sold his business to his best friend. We would have gone out for Chinese, because that's what we did for family celebrations.

I never saw money as something to worry about or imagined that saving for retirement would be hard. And growing up in a very close-knit family, I absorbed my parents' values.

The golden nugget: my dad's strategy

I was about nine years old when Dad retired. This is going back 40 years. I think he did well. He was 65 and sold his business and invested that money.

Yes, eventually he invested, but that's only because he'd always been a saver and knew he needed to do something with the money.

Sure, someone else might have taken the kind of money he earned over the years and bought a property with it earlier on, or bought shares. But he just invested it in a long-term bank account and he had the interest coming in, probably quarterly.

We lived on the interest from his investments, which wasn't a lot—it would have been several thousand dollars. But it was enough to support our whole family at the time. My parents never spent the principal. That was the point. It's a bit like buying a property and never selling it: you live off the rent; you don't sell the principal asset.

> Don't sell your principal asset. It will continue to experience growth and needs to be held to provide the income.

The money taboo

My parents were set up reasonably well because Dad had some investment money and his veteran's pension, which meant Mum had a bit of money to retire on, and there was their principal place of residence, the mortgage-free farmhouse.

None of this was consciously taught to me. Actually, money was never spoken about. Mum used to admonish us, 'Money is the root of all evil.' I heard this aphorism often when we were kids, though I didn't really understand what it meant.

Maybe it was an inherited belief. Frugality was a quality ingrained in many born during the war years or earlier.

Open discussion of money, salaries, debt and wealth is a recent trend, yet even today money is considered by many to be a taboo topic. A 2024 Bankrate survey found that Americans consider talk about money as more taboo than talking about politics, religion or a person's weight.

I frequently argue that while, to turn to another familiar saying, 'money can't buy happiness', it can buy choices and security.

A cash stash

One firm belief I inherited from my parents, and still hold to be true, is that you need to keep some cash in the bank. A lot of people question this idea, pointing out that cash loses value over time, and therefore, they say, you should invest everything in assets that will appreciate. While that is true in principle, you should always have some cash available because you never know what is around the corner.

Investing comes later. Initially, you need to set some money aside in your freedom fund.

Being asset-rich and cash-poor means you're not set up properly, because if some unexpected expense crops up, you need to know the money's there to cover it.

While writing this our Boston terrier Frankie came down with tick paralysis after a trip to our holiday home on the south coast. She ended up being put on a ventilator, and we almost lost her.

Frankie: one of the family

The vet bill for one day was $7000. Paying it was a no-brainer as Frankie is part of our family, but we also had access, as always, to our cash stash.

I've never really believed in pet insurance. Frankie did recover, and we brought her home after seven days in the veterinary hospital, but I never expected a vet bill of $50 000 — that's almost a house deposit!

I plan to buy insurance now.

The importance of accessible cash

You may be a multi-millionaire on paper. But in an emergency, you can't just get money out of your house. It takes time. You either sell, which might take months, or refinance, and that too takes time. Even shares, which are more liquid, take time to turn into cash. You've got to sell them and then access your money a few days later.

So those who invest all their cash are going too far. I think you need to do both. Personally, I feel wealthier when I've got access to some cash. I remember that even at age 20 I felt uncomfortable without some money in the bank, and I'm still like that now. I have money in the bank now that I won't touch.

Of course it all begins with self-education and setting saving strategies, which are the subjects of the next chapter.

Key takeaways

- Investing in property can set you up for life.
- But first you need to know your why, to set a passive income goal and to develop an investment strategy to achieve it.
- Being asset-rich and cash-poor means you're not set up properly, because when some unexpected expense crops up, you need to know the money's there to cover it.
- Initially you need to build a freedom fund — investing comes later.
- Your freedom fund is a backup account that will, first, cover any unexpected costs and, then, hold assets that generate cash flow to enable you to retire when you want to and live the life you want to.

Chapter 2

Save for your first and only deposit

Growing up, I didn't think much about money because we always had enough, but when I moved away from home it became a source of stress.

I was 19 when I moved from central NSW to Sydney to enrol at the Sydney Conservatorium of Music. This had been a lifelong dream for me—I'd practised my trombone for hours every day and had even given up competitive golf to get to the Con. My family was so proud. I adapted pretty well. I didn't know a lot of people but I had a couple of friends at the Con I'd met at music competitions around the state when I was at high school.

Many of my fellow students came from Sydney and lived at home so their living expenses were covered. I'd moved from Orange to Erskineville in Sydney and of course I had to pay my way. Although Austudy wasn't a loan back then, it was means-tested. The amount I received covered my rent but left nothing for food or petrol, let alone clothes. I supplemented my grant money with a little teaching and a few gigs, but my earnings didn't go far and for the first time I experienced money stress.

I'd buy a daily ticket and catch the train in to the Con. If I could scrape together $3.80, I'd buy Chinese Mongolian lamb for dinner at the Erskineville Chinese takeaway. It may have been 'cheap and nasty' but it tasted pretty good, and it was cheaper for me to do that than buy groceries to cook at home. That was my only lifestyle spending, apart from renting a cheap place in a nice part of town.

Then everything changed.

One weekend the band was given a gig in Newcastle, about three hours' drive north. I needed the cash. I had nothing in my wallet, and four days before my Austudy payment came through. But I couldn't afford to put petrol in my petrol-guzzling XD Ford Falcon with 500 000 kilometres on the clock.

I had to turn the job down and let someone else take my place.

I couldn't go anywhere that weekend. I was stuck in my apartment with no food and no money. And no Mongolian lamb. I could do nothing for four days except walk around with a grumbling tummy. It felt terrible, and brought home to me how much I needed money in the bank, not just for rent and bills but also for emergencies. My mindset around money changed forever.

That was the start of the financial discipline I still maintain. I never wanted to be in a position where I had no money. So the next time I got paid I saved something.

Saving just $20 freed me from the misery of the week before, when I'd had nothing. The next time it was maybe $100. When I had $200 in the bank, I started to relax again. I determined I wouldn't be turning down any gigs or going hungry for four days anytime soon.

The next time I got paid, I saved more; $500 became $1000, and I felt increasingly comfortable. And then I had $2000 in the bank and felt better than I had the previous month. And then it was $5000. And I was growing that. Now I was in the fortunate position of being able to do fun things when I wanted to. I could buy jet skis or spend money on cars, whatever.

When I was 25 and had $5000 in the bank I felt rich. These days, if I had only $5000 in my account I'd feel poor. As you get older you set yourself up for more.

Even today I always consider what 'discretionary money' we have available before I go out and spend on stuff. And I'll make sure that every time I splurge on something, I'm also saving money somewhere. All the time.

You can't save your way to wealth

I know saving money can be trickier for some people than for others. Impulse control is a big one for people with any neurodivergence, for example. We'll talk more about that in chapter 3.

I myself have a bit of OCD—otherwise known as obsessive compulsive disorder. For me, it is manifested by having really high standards and being unable to let things go. So when I was a music student and had no money and was living on McDonald's ice-cream and couldn't afford petrol, I'd felt terrible.

Once I was putting something aside from each pay cheque I was determined not to go backwards. And so it went.

Over the next seven years my savings grew from zero to $30 000. That was a lot back then. During those years of saving through the back half of the 1990s and early 2000s I never went on overseas holidays, never had a credit card, and never bought a new car or fancy clothes.

In 2003 that freedom fund became the deposit on my one-bedroom unit in Rockdale, near the airport in Sydney. I used the $30 000 I had, and with stamp duty and other costs it came to about $40 000 in total.

Once I had bought the Rockdale apartment, compounding growth kicked in.

After a while, though, I realised that though the income I was now earning as a music teacher at Moriah College was enough to pay my mortgage on a one-bedroom unit, it wouldn't be enough to provide real security for me in the future.

Because you can't save yourself to wealth. That's the whole point of investing.

What I'd tell my younger self

Einstein described compound interest as the eighth wonder of the world (turn to chapter 4 for more). He was right! As to my first investment strategies, what I'd probably do differently with that $30 000 freedom fund is to *rentvest*.

My Rockdale apartment was probably a 20-minute drive from Moriah College. My second property, in Ingleburn, necessitated a really long commute, but I already knew it was just a stepping stone.

That's why I advise people these days to rentvest—in other words, rent a property you're comfortable living in that is close to your work and, if possible, close to the sort of facilities that support the lifestyle you choose. Then buy another property, just to get onto the property investment ladder—but make your first property purchase an investment property in a location you can afford and, more important, a property that is a better type of investment.

With 20/20 hindsight, I'd probably still have lived in Rockdale but I wouldn't have bought there. I'd have rented there and probably bought an investment property in another state.

Rockdale did okay for me, but it wasn't ideal. It was my first property, but at no point have I said it was a good investment property. I was pretty lucky with it because it was well located—close to the train line, close to cafés, close to the water. Truthfully, though, that was all by chance.

It was also an apartment, not a house. So it wasn't a very good investment property in terms of performance. A standalone house will grow in value faster. So that's probably what I'd advise a younger me to do now.

At the time it was comparatively cheap to buy in Queensland. For the same money as I spent on purchasing the Rockdale apartment, I could have bought a decent house in Brisbane or regional Queensland, and it would have been a better long-term investment.

My inspiration: rich kids I taught

So my wealth-creation aspirations began when I was at Moriah College teaching students from well-off families. I was never jealous; I used to look at them and think, how did these people get to live in those really big houses with swimming pools? How can they drive such expensive cars and send their kids to the most expensive schools in Sydney? And how do I get there too?

I've always been interested in how someone starting out without much money — in my case, a bank balance of $20 000 and a salary of $50 000 — can elevate themselves. That's what actually got me going: the feeling of 'I want to have all that one day'. But I also realised I wouldn't *get* all that by sitting around complaining — or by staying in the teaching profession and not getting paid much.

How I educated myself

I began to educate myself by reading books like this one. Yes, I read Robert Kiyosaki's *Rich Dad, Poor Dad,* which really opened my eyes to ways of thinking about money and assets.

I attended a lot of seminars — including some bad ones! In those days, lots of spruikers put on free seminars and tried to sell you terrible house-and-land packages or off-the-plan units. These days you'll find a lot of tried and tested information out there, and less dodgy stuff.

I subscribed to property magazines and read everything I could get my hands on. And once YouTube took off I started looking at content there. (Now I produce my own content! And books, of course.)

Today I have enough passive income from property to retire on. But I love what I do. I love meeting people and hearing what they want to achieve. I love listening to their goals and dreams and it means so much to me to be a part of that. I can also increase my philanthropic work, as I have the means to do that. I'll discuss this more in chapter 12.

I'm fortunate to have a business that gives me the flexibility to spend as much time as I want having perfect days with my kids, as my own father did. I'm a bit of an older dad, too, so I've had time to set things up financially so I can spend time with my kids. And Renee works part-time because she chooses to.

Time with my family fills my cup, but if I didn't work I'd become bored. I'm high-functioning and I love doing stuff that adds value to the world. That's my purpose. In other words, work too fills my cup.

What I want for everyone who reads this book is that same freedom to choose how you spend your time and your money. It's still about peace of mind. Knowing your freedom fund is there, so you can also just enjoy what you can afford and be happy along the way, without stressing about how many properties you own or how much money you have.

Of course my lifestyle is different now from when I was 20, but my attitude hasn't changed. These days I try to save about half my salary. Because I don't spend much and I earn a fair bit, I can put a fair bit aside. Fifty per cent is probably too much for many people, but I recommend you try to save at least 10 to 15 per cent of your weekly income, bearing in mind that you may also have costs such as mortgages, rent, school fees and the like.

Pay yourself first

Set yourself a non-negotiable weekly saving amount. Be realistic. You can always add to your freedom fund but you don't want to fall short of the weekly amount you've set.

Lloyd's strategy

Live below your means

The principle is the same whether you earn $60 000 or $400 000 a year.

Set up an automatic transfer to put 10 per cent straight into savings/investments on payday. Put money to cover your fixed costs (mortgage, bills) in a separate account. What's left is yours to spend — guilt-free.

To make things more achievable, start small and build momentum:

- *Week 1:* Put $100 into the bank.
- *Week 4:* Aim for $400.
- *Month 3:* Hit $1500.
- *Month 12:* Reach $6000.

The key is consistency: set that money aside in a separate bank account and don't touch it. It's your freedom fund.

Set up automatic transfers on your phone, *before* you can spend it:

- Transfer $5 to $20 a day into a separate savings account.
- Round up your savings by setting up a system that rounds up every purchase you make to the nearest dollar: then put the difference into savings. You'll hardly notice, but every cent helps.
- Set up a system so 10 per cent of every pay cheque you receive automatically goes into savings before you even see it. That's the payday split.

Automatic savings

Ask your bank to alert you every time you save $25 and every time you reach a savings milestone.

Your phone can be your savings helper. Set up goals in your banking app with progress bars. Watching those bars fill up triggers the same reward pathways as those triggered by shopping—but you're building wealth instead of debt.

Set up these features today.

Visual progress tracking

Create multiple savings accounts with exciting names, such as:

- Property Deposit Fund
- Never Ordering Takeaway Again Fund
- Financial Freedom Fund
- Emergency Buffer Fund.

Australian banking app features

Here's what the major Australian banks offer.

CommBank

- Benefits Finder identifies government benefits for which you're eligible.
- Spending Tracker categorises spending automatically.
- Lock/Block Card freezes your card when you're tempted.

NAB

- NAB Spaces offers virtual savings 'buckets' with custom names.
- Spending Insights shows where your money goes.
- Bill Smoothing predicts upcoming bills.

ANZ

- Save the Change rounds up purchases and saves the difference.
- Money Tracker gives real-time spending notifications.

Westpac

- Spend Tracker provides visual charts of your spending patterns.
- Savings Goals lets you set targets and gives you progress bars.
- Impulse Saver lets you transfer money to savings before you can spend it.

ING

- Everyday Round Up enables automatic savings from rounded-up transactions.
- Sub-accounts lets you create up to nine savings accounts with different goals.

Up Banking

- Savers offers unlimited mini savings accounts with custom emojis.
- Instant notifications notifies you of every transaction (immediate feedback).
- Up Insights shows you your real-time spending with colourful visuals.

How to pay off debt

If you have debts to clear before you can start saving, you will have to do more than make the minimum payments. Try the smallest debt first for motivation—this is known as the Snowball method. Then go for the Avalanche method, which involves paying down those that attract the highest interest. You'll need to reduce discretionary spending and try to increase income to accelerate the payoff.

Lloyd's strategy

The three-bucket system

No matter what you earn, use this system and automate it on your phone. I'll keep it simple.

Bucket 1: Needs (50 to 60 per cent of income)

- mortgage/rent
- bills and utilities
- groceries
- transport
- insurances
- minimum debt repayments.

Bucket 2: Savings and investments (20 to 30 per cent of income)

- emergency fund (aim to cover six months' worth of expenses)
- property deposit(s)
- share investments
- extra debt repayments
- superannuation top-ups.

(continued)

Bucket 3: Wants (20 to 30 per cent of income)

- entertainment
- dining out
- holidays
- hobbies
- self-care and fun.

Should you get a pay rise or an income boost, increase your savings rate (Bucket 2), not your spending rate. If your raise is $10 000, put $5000 into extra savings/investments. Only then put money into Bucket 3.

It's what you keep

It's not how much you earn; it's how much you keep and how much you can make what you keep work for you.

I've met tradies who earn $80 000 a year but have a $2 million property portfolio. And I've met executives who earn $300 000 and are living pay cheque to pay cheque.

While it's great that most of us are saving something and that we're saving more this year than we did last year, most of us don't have enough to draw on in a crisis, and that's a real concern.

The bottom line is that saving is crucial to financial freedom. If you want to enjoy security and, eventually, financial freedom by getting into property, you'll need a decent deposit. And, as I've suggested, you also need a buffer for unforeseen events.

Forming good habits around budgeting, saving and smart, timely investing will allow you to achieve true wealth and true freedom.

That means having well-managed income streams providing passive income that enable you to lead your best life.

In time, as you continue to save and invest, you'll amass assets that will not only enable you to live your dream but also to spread the wealth by helping others and so leave a positive mark on the world.

The alternative approach

The goal isn't to *look* rich; the goal is to *be* wealthy. There's a difference. Truly wealthy people live well, but not for show.

- They have a nice house, but it doesn't need to be the biggest on the street.
- They own good cars, but not the newest luxury models.
- They take holidays, but not constantly.
- They invest in quality goods, not flashy showpieces.

They have buffers:

- six to 12 months' expenses in cash
- income from multiple sources
- paid-off or low-debt assets
- insurance.

They buy assets, not liabilities:

- investment properties that pay them rather than costing them
- shares that pay dividends
- businesses that generate cash flow
- additional superannuation (for tax benefits).

Delayed gratification

Delaying gratification in this world of instant indulgence and the seductions of new technologies is a true achievement, whether you're resisting your own desires or those of your children.

The seduction of the latest tech is part of the problem. When I was growing up in Orange in the 1980s, there were no mobile phones or social media. We had a Commodore computer on which we could play 'Snake'. That was it.

As children we played outdoors. I first sat on a horse when I was two years old. As a kid I used to wake up and ride my horse or my motorbike around the property with my next-door neighbour before school. It was great. Yes, we had horses and motorbikes, but the bikes were secondhand.

No-one judged anyone by the vehicle they drove in Orange—unless they drove an expensive car! We all drove utes or old trucks. There wasn't a thing about brand-new cars or keeping up with what everyone else had.

Sure, we all like new things: a shiny new car or a jet ski or the latest iPhone—but you don't need these things when you're 21 and trying to save money with your long-term future in mind. Banking technologies like credit cards facilitate instant gratification. I was 36 before I had my first credit card. Sure, today such activities as booking tickets, flights and hotels pretty much require a card, but be aware of the dangers of impulse buying.

I also don't think you need an instant-gratification app like Afterpay, which allows you to buy now and pay later. That isn't the way to get ahead because it encourages you to take on debt.

It's important to maintain a balance, and that means setting yourself up with two bank accounts: a spending account and a savings account. You need to save more than you spend.

Then, with the money you're saving, look at how you can invest that to create more wealth. You might be saving the deposit for a home—not a home you're going to live in but the best investment property you can afford at the time.

Now I'll introduce you to some budgeting strategies to help you maintain that balance.

Our sons, Riley and Caelen, are still babies—seven and five years old—but I'm already teaching them these lessons. I give Riley $5 and have him decide what to do with it. He can spend it all on ice-cream, or he can save it to buy something bigger later on, like a toy. Neither of my kids spends money at the moment—they put it into their piggy banks.

That's where it starts. Teaching kids the value of money from a young age. Because they're not going to learn this at school. They'll learn Pythagoras's theorem, but not how to set up a proper budget when they move out of home.

Key takeaways

- Work backwards from a passive income goal, living off interest and rent.
- Discover the rewards of saving and the magic of compound interest for growth.
- Rentvesting allows you to step onto the property investment ladder while living in a rental where you choose.
- Seize every opportunity for self-education through property books and magazines, podcasts and seminars.
- Form good habits around saving and set yourself saving strategies.
- Delay instant gratification so you can grow that freedom fund and start saving toward your first and only deposit.

Chapter 3

Hack your budget to save money

If you are a beginner saver, you might need some budgeting inspiration, whether you're starting your freedom fund or paying down your mortgages. It's going to mean facing your own spending weaknesses and outsmarting yourself.

Coffee: my weakness

When it comes to budgeting, I talk a lot about resisting avocado toast and Uber Eats and credit cards. But I have had my weaknesses.

For me, it was food—specifically, takeaway food—and coffee. When I lived in Erskineville, Redfern and Rockdale, Sydney's amazing food scene was a constant temptation.

I never drank coffee as a kid. My mum used to love instant coffee; I never liked the taste. But when I went to the Conservatorium, everyone was sipping lattes. It was the thing to do. For me it was really nice—but I couldn't afford it.

I know — I'm always telling people they should budget for takeaway and café coffees, and I struggled with that myself. I didn't like making coffee at home. Even now, I'd rather go out and buy a latte.

I'm still obsessed with coffee. It's what I have for breakfast. Now we've got an expensive coffee machine at home that I bought for Renee. But she still asks me to bring her one from the café! But, honestly, we used to have a cheap Aldi pod machine and I think it made better coffee than our $1500 espresso machine.

I could have been budgeting better and not spending on café lattes or an espresso machine, especially since I prefer Aldi coffee anyway.

The trade-off

Budgeting is all about finding a balance between today and your perfect day. It's all about what coffee means to you and whether it's worth the expense.

For example, buying a coffee might mean something different if you work from home. If you're working from home, you're saving transport costs by not commuting. You might be saving more in petrol than you spend on coffee.

Maybe buying that ridiculous seven-dollar coffee and spending time in a café is actually your time out, your one hit of social time. You can give yourself that small reward because you're saving money elsewhere.

In other words, I'm not saying everybody should stop buying café coffee. It's just an example to get you thinking about your expenses and where you can save.

For my staff I have a 100 per cent work-from-home policy. Renee and I prefer to work in the office, but having no-one else there works well because we don't get distracted. Some of my team live 45 minutes to an hour away from the office. Not commuting saves so much time. They can log in earlier; they can log off later. Instead of shutting the laptop at five because they've got to get home, they might stay logged on until six because they're already home.

Productivity is better, and they're saving travel costs. Because they're not coming to the office, their social time might be going to the café or the gym. It's a net gain.

Don't buy the jet ski with your savings

Everybody has their weakness. Just be honest with yourself. Whatever your savings kryptonite may be, make sure you're not spending all your discretionary income on it. Balance smart saving with judicious spending. Don't attempt to deprive yourself completely, but don't let small indulgences derail your greater financial goals.

I do buy birthday presents for Renee and I did buy jet skis for the family last summer, but not everyone's going to be buying jet skis. Not everyone lives on the water and not everyone has the necessary disposable income.

For example, if you've got the $20 000 in savings you'd need, would you be better off putting that towards a deposit on a property?

Or if you're a homeowner, would it be smarter to put $20 000 in your mortgage offset account since that would help pay down the interest and in turn help you accrue more equity—savings you could put towards a deposit on another asset, such as an investment property?

So if $20 000 is all you've got, buying a jet ski is not the best use of that money, even if it's fun. You need to try to build up your freedom fund first.

Although I now have a passive income from 16 properties and a business, when I spend money to buy things I check to make sure it's within my means. If I'm going to buy this handbag for Renee, or if I'm going to buy this jet ski, I think, okay, that's going to cost this much, but I can still put this much away.

Put your $20 000 into your freedom fund for that house deposit or for paying down your housing loan. It doesn't mean you have to pay the whole house off before you can buy anything frivolous. But once you've put down more—say, $60 000—toward paying for the house, then you might be able to reward yourself and buy a jet ski, or a new eco-friendly car, because you've also got money in your offset account. You can withdraw money from the offset should you need it, which means you've got money you can have fun with without wasting cash.

It's about balance: making sure you've got money going into paying off your house and that you're in a comfortable position financially before you spend big on non-appreciating assets.

Of course, a secondhand jet ski is always an option; you don't have to buy a new one. You can pick up a secondhand one for $6000, though it's probably been underwater at some point so you shouldn't expect it to work perfectly.

It all comes back to your perfect day. If it's about creating fun summer memories with the family, you don't need to go big. Renee has a paddleboard, and we've got kayaks. We had the kayaks long before we bought the jet skis. A kayak can cost as little as $200, and not only do you get out on the water, you get exercise as well.

Remember the '$400 000 earner' rule:

- If you earn $200 000 a year and live as though you earn $400 000 you're building stress.
- If you earn $400 000 and live as though you earn $200 000, you're building wealth.

Use a budget planner

Other items you need to watch are those small but regular weekly expenditures. You're probably not going to save the equivalent of the cost of a jet ski out of your weekly income, but you might save a few hundred a month by using Uber Eats less often or by skipping the Friday night Indian. Instead, cook at home and save the $80. Over six months (26 weeks x $80), you'll save thousands of dollars, for all that $80 may be a small percentage of your weekly income.

If you have trouble saving, a good budget planner, in which you list your income and living expenses, can make all the difference. A basic Excel spreadsheet will do the trick (see table 3.1, overleaf). Or search for a good budget-tracking app.

Check and update your planner weekly to help you track your spending and ensure you're sticking to your goals. Make this a habit.

Table 3.1 *budget planner*

View: Annual			
Income	**$**	**Frequency**	**$**
Your take-home pay		Fortnightly	
Income from savings/ investments		Monthly	
Other income		Monthly	
Home and utilities	**$**	**Frequency**	**$**
Mortgage or rent		Monthly	
Council rates		Quarterly	
Electricity, gas and water		Quarterly	
Internet, pay TV, phone		Monthly	
Other		Monthly	
Insurance and financial	**$**	**Frequency**	**$**
Car insurance		Monthly	
Home and contents insurance		Monthly	
Personal, life and health insurance		Monthly	
Loans		Monthly	
Other		Monthly	
Groceries and personal	**$**	**Frequency**	**$**
Supermarket		Weekly	
Education and school fees		Quarterly	
Sports and fitness		Weekly	
Entertainment and eating out		Weekly	
Other		Weekly	
Transport and auto	**$**	**Frequency**	**$**
Bus, train, ferry or taxi		Weekly	
Petrol		Weekly	
Road tolls and parking		Weekly	

View: Annual			
Income	**$**	**Frequency**	**$**
Rego and licence		Yearly	
Other		Weekly	
Summary			
	Monthly totals		
	Home and utilities	$	
	Insurance and financial	$	
	Groceries and personal	$	
	Transport and auto	$	

The bottom line

The average Australian spending $50 a week on Uber Eats could save $2600 every year by cooking at home instead. Unused subscriptions and memberships cost many of us up to $2000 a year. Add in impulse online shopping and that total can rise by thousands of dollars more.

All these impulse spends may not seem like much—until you add them up. Even small expenditures, if they're frequent enough, can add up to thousands or tens of thousands of dollars in a year.

As an exercise, calculate what you spend on small stuff, from takeaways to not-so-bargain buys to subscriptions, in an average week. Then multiply that sum by 52. That's potentially thousands of dollars, a big chunk of a deposit that could be the start of a property portfolio.

It makes you see all those impulse spends in a different light.

Make cooking fun

The average Uber Eats order for one person costs somewhere between $30 and $50. The same meal cooked at home costs between $8 and $15. The trick is to make cooking fun:

- Shop online for the ingredients and have them delivered.
- Put on your favourite music or podcast.
- Cook with the kids or with a friend over video call.
- On Sundays, meal-prep and freeze 'fast food' for the whole week.
- Try new recipes as a challenge.
- Use home cooking to help meet your health goals.
- Calculate the money you're saving each time.

Every time you cook at home instead of ordering in, transfer the 'delivery fee' of $5, or even the whole $30, to your savings account, and watch your property deposit grow.

Understand what's really happening

What you need to understand about impulse buying is that often you're not shopping because you need x, y or z. Your brain is seeking the instant chemical reward that buying or winning stuff gives you. Though most of us have a bunch of rationalisations for impulse spending, a lot of us are doing it essentially for the dopamine hit.

These days you don't even need to leave home to shop. Online shopping sites and apps, including food delivery and gambling apps, are designed to exploit your brain's vulnerabilities, using every marketing trick in the book to get you to buy whatever it is they're selling.

Renee definitely falls for these tactics. She doesn't actually waste money. She buys something only if she is convinced there's value in it. But if she sees something that's half price, she often feels she has to buy it.

This is a false economy because that sale item isn't really half price. At first, the retailer inflates the price substantially before announcing it's going on sale. And it works. What many of us don't realise is that the strategic person here is the retailer, not the shopper.

The rule of thumb here is if you don't need it and/or love it, don't buy it just because it's 'on sale'.

Lloyd's strategy

Drop shopping

Before making a non-essential purchase over $50, try the following.

The 30-day rule

Add the desired item to a wish list, then close the app. Wait 30 days. If you still want it, and you've saved the money to pay for it, consider buying it. Especially if it's now 'on sale'.

Make the 'hourly wage' calculation

Calculate how many hours you'll need to work (after tax) to pay for the desired item. A $500 purchase if you earn $30 per hour after tax equals 16.7 hours of your life. Is it worth it?

(continued)

Ask the 'opportunity cost' question

Ask yourself, *What else could this money do?* If the purchase would cost you $500, it could also buy you:

- a hefty contribution to your freedom fund
- part of a deposit on an investment
- part of a deposit on an investment property that will appreciate over time.

Take the 'joy' test

Ask yourself, Will this still be likely to bring me joy in six months' time? Or will it just make me happy in this moment? Be honest with yourself. (Note: most impulse purchases fail this test!)

Discover sustainable vintage fashion

Here's one I really like: op shopping. You get to bargain hunt, you're helping a charity — and you're out of the house and off your phone. Salvos, Good Sammy, Vinnies, Red Cross — they're all worth a visit. It's a great dopamine hit when you snare a bargain, and it's even tax deductible.

Decide beforehand how much you can spend and take only that amount, in cash. That means when the money is gone, you're done.

Beloved by Gen Z and teenagers, top online secondhand clothes-selling platforms include Depop, Vinted, Poshmark and Vestiaire Collective.

Sell your stuff

You can make money by selling retro and new tech, hobby equipment, tools, musical instruments, sporting goods, designer clothes, collectors' items and jewellery. One room at a time, sort stuff into boxes to keep, trash, donate or sell. Be ruthless. If you haven't worn or used it in a year, and it doesn't bring you joy, into the box.

Then list the items saleable online — at, say, eBay, Facebook Marketplace or Gumtree. You could also take quality clothes in good nick to secondhand dealers. This does take time and storage space, including trips to the post office.

As well as giving you a dopamine hit, selling all that stuff you barely use will not just help grow your freedom fund but will free up living space. You'll start to feel on track with your budgeting goals and more confident about saving.

Lloyd's golden rule

Match every discretionary purchase you make with equivalent savings. Want to spend $100 on something fun? Great. But $100 goes into your savings first. This way you're never depleting your wealth. You're building it, while still enjoying life.

Lloyd's strategy

Delete the apps

This is your first and most important step. I'm serious about this. Remember your goal and treat it as a 'for now' step to help you budget for 30 days.

(continued)

Delete now:

- food delivery apps
- online shopping apps
- gambling apps (use BetStop — the Australian Government's National Self-Exclusion Register)
- saved payment methods from websites.

Why this works, especially if you have a neurospicy brain

Adding friction between impulse and action gives your prefrontal cortex time to engage. ADHD brains benefit from structured systems that minimise snap decisions.

Turn on budgeting pings

My banking app on my phone alerts me every time money is spent, whether by me or by anyone else using the company credit card. It also tells me exactly how much I've spent. It itemises what we've spent that month on entertainment, going out, food or whatever. And that's really interesting.

For people who are budgeting, a good banking app is an excellent tool to show you where your money is going. It also alerts me when money is coming in.

Turn ON dopamine-spiking notifications for:

- money coming in (every deposit, pay, refund)
- savings milestones ('You've saved $500!')
- round-up totals ('You've saved $27.50 this week!')
- goal progress ('You've reached 70 per cent of your emergency fund goal!').

Chop up your credit card

A lot of people get themselves into debt through overusing credit cards. If you're that sort of person, get yourself a debit card. It does the same thing as a credit card except it won't let you spend money you don't have. Get rid of the credit cards then add repayments for any outstanding credit card debt into your budget planner.

Lloyd's strategy

The subscription audit

Most Australians waste between $50 and $200 a month on forgotten subscriptions. Time to delete them all and get a dopamine rush from the savings you'll make!

Find them all

Check your bank app's subscription tracker. Look for recurring charges from things such as:

- video streaming platforms
- shopping platforms
- gaming subscriptions
- gym memberships and classes you don't use
- meal kits you forgot about.

Delete ruthlessly

Keep *only* what you have used in the past seven days. Consider sharing accounts with friends or family (splitting a Netflix or Amazon subscription instead of everyone paying separately).

(continued)

Cancel gym memberships you don't use often enough to justify the ongoing expense. Instead, go for a run or do free fitness classes online.

Delete those pricey meal kits: you can cook from scratch for a quarter of the price.

Track the savings

Do the sums and you'll see just how much you could be adding to your monthly savings by scrapping unnecessary memberships and subscriptions. We ditched:

- Netflix ($18 per month)
- gym membership fees ($60 per month)
- HelloFresh ($198 per month)
- total monthly savings: $276.

Transferred into your savings account each month, this money would grow to a healthy $3312 by year's end.

Turn off money sucking pings

Yes, turn those social and spending phone notifications off — everything except calls. You're not actually ignoring your apps if you don't answer straight away. You can give yourself specific times to check your phone every day so you don't miss anything important.

When you have notifications on for Instagram and Facebook, you have to scroll through a huge number of ads. Even when you're watching someone on Instagram, an ad will pop up and you're hooked. Then there are the influencers, all of whom are selling something.

If you need to delete these apps for 30 days until the savings habit is entrenched and you stop going down wormholes, do it. Drastic times call for drastic measures.

Free dopamine boosters

The key isn't merely to stop impulse spending. It's a whole shift in habits. That requires willpower, and willpower can fail us. The key is to replace our dopamine-seeking buying behaviours with cheaper, healthier alternatives that bring the same brain-chemical reward, as well as protecting our freedom fund balance.

About to spend money online buying something you don't need? Outsmart yourself with a distraction! Go look at some cute cats or a baby dressed up as a banana. Or do something active, fun and free. Don't multitask. Let yourself do one thing at a time.

Quick hits (two to five minutes)

- Take box breaths: in 2, 3, 4—hold 2, 3, 4—out 2, 3, 4—hold 2, 3, 4 …
- Splash your face with cold water.
- Watch cute animal videos (yes, seriously).
- Do some jumping jacks, pillow punches or sit-ups to your favourite song (or just dance).
- Get sunshine on your face—take a quick stroll in the fresh air.
- Cuddle or play with your pet.
- Text a friend a funny meme and make plans.
- Make a cup of tea, paying attention to all five senses.

Make rewards visible

Keep a 'deposit jar' on the kitchen bench. Every time you feel the urge to spend on your bad habit, take what you would have spent if you'd given in to that urge out of your wallet and put it in the jar. You'll soon see how much ditching your habits contributes to increasing your freedom fund or buying an investment property.

Big hits (20 to 60 minutes)

- Go for a walk, a run, a dip, a surf, a SUP, a kayak. Twenty minutes of exercise outside can lower stress hormones, and going barefoot in nature is grounding.
- Hit the gym: a guaranteed dopamine hit. Leisure centres, pools and some gyms are budget-friendly.
- Phone a friend for a good chin wag.
- Do a guided meditation (phone on *do not disturb*).
- Play a card or board game with family or friends.
- Get creative: bake, draw, colour, journal, play an instrument, cook a meal.
- Do a spot of gardening—or repot a houseplant or two.
- Browse the library or a book store—finish this book first!

The social connection factor

Social connection is free and offers one of the most powerful dopamine hits. Studies reveal dopamine levels rise significantly more when you interact with another person rather than with a computer screen. Surprise, surprise.

Scrap solo scrolling

- Schedule regular video calls with mates—one on one or group chats.
- Meet for walks with BYO coffee rather than meeting in pricey cafes.
- Attend free community events.
- Sign up for a course that involves group classes.
- Join and participate in online support and/or neighbourhood networking groups.
- Volunteer.

Gain momentum

When you open your phone, instead of shopping apps you'll see your growing bank balance. And because you've found less expensive ways to meet your entertainment, food and fitness needs, you won't feel deprived. Win–win.

Share your wins with a friend to shore up accountability.

Calculate the total you've saved this month and compare it to what you saved the previous month. If you've saved more, celebrate. Have a 'perfect hour' or, if you can, a perfect afternoon or a whole perfect day.

If you're paying down mortgage debt, extra savings left over after the month's living expenses can be put in the offset account. This can have an amazing compounding effect. I saw this firsthand when we had a mortgage on our home.

Lloyd's strategy

What success looks like

You'll know these habits are working when:

- you open your banking app more often than your social media apps
- you get excited as you watch your savings grow
- before buying something you automatically ask yourself what you could do with the money instead
- you are happy to cook at home
- you choose free activities because you genuinely enjoy them, not just to save money
- your first thought when you get paid is *how much can I save?* rather than *what can I buy?*
- you have three to six months of expenses saved
- you've started looking at investment properties.

If you keep this up for a month, you'll have reprogrammed your brain to associate your phone with saving money rather than spending it. You'll have begun to establish healthy new habits around spending and saving. And you'll have begun to see there are lots of free, feel-good ways to have fun.

Best of all, you'll have extra money in the bank.

That's when you know you've rewired your brain. And that's when you're on the path to real wealth. When you're saving and investing you're building wealth, for yourself and for your family, so you can make a positive difference in the world.

You are well on your way to growing that freedom fund. Next we'll talk about how to maximise your gains.

Key takeaways

- Budgeting is all about finding a balance between today and your perfect day.
- It's making sure you've got money going into paying off your house and you're in a comfortable position financially *before* you spend big on non-appreciating assets.
- If you have trouble saving, a good budget planner, in which you list your income and living expenses, can make you see all those impulse spends in a different light.
- Match every discretionary purchase you make with equivalent savings.
- Ditch all those unused or underused apps and conduct a rigorous subscription audit.

Chapter 4

Double your money through compound interest

Once you've learned how to budget properly and you've started taking back control of your finances, you can move into the part of the process where the magic of investing in order to double your money happens.

Saving and managing money are important, but how can we take what we have and grow it? In this chapter we'll explore what is really the crux of property investing. With property we can leverage our money so the income we earn can grow into something much bigger.

One of the most common goals of the clients who come to me is wanting to double their money through property.

You might be looking at the property market and asking yourself, *how does anyone double their money anymore?* Especially when prices seem high, interest rates are unpredictable and every headline expresses a different opinion on what the future holds.

Doubling your money in property is still possible, not through luck or timing but through *time in the market*. Time in the market allows for compounding growth. It's also the right strategy and will set you up for life, if you buy well and in the right markets.

When I bought my first property in Rockdale in 2003, I had no idea how dramatically the compounding growth in its value would change my financial future. I just knew I wanted something better than scraping together $3.80 for Chinese Mongolian lamb in Erskineville.

This is what I want to explore in this chapter: how do property markets actually move and how can you read the cycles and position yourself to benefit from them over the long term.

The key to wealth creation through property

At its core, successful property investment relies on capital growth; that is, the linear increase in a property's value over time. When a property grows in value, your equity — the difference between what the property is worth and what you owe on it — increases.

The faster your growth rate, the faster your equity will grow. This will allow you to leverage that equity to purchase more properties and build your portfolio faster.

Property growth vs savings

If you get a job and work for 40 years, you are not really creating wealth. It may be different if you are very highly paid — as a highly sought-after brain surgeon, say. If you're on an average income, you can't save your way to wealth.

Let's say you're earning $100 000 after tax and your expenses total $80 000. You're paying rent or making mortgage repayments and covering all the other expenses, such as food.

You've got $20 000 left at the end of the year.

Let's say you saved that $20 000 and you saved a further $20 000 the following year and succeeding years. You could work for five years and save $100 000. That seems like a good chunk of savings given that a lot of people have less than $1000 in the bank, right?

You could invest your way to wealth with that $100 000 because the good thing about property is that *it grows in value* if it's in the right location.

Doubling your money comes down to compounding growth. It's an equation: if you get 7.2 per cent growth a year on your property, compounding over 10 years, your property will double in value over that period.

The rule of 72: double your equity in a decade

To calculate what annual growth rate is needed to double your property's value within a decade, investors apply 'the Rule of 72', which is based on the following formula:

72 ÷ annual growth rate = number of years to double

According to the rule of 72, then, your property needs to grow by approximately 7.2 per cent a year, on average, over 10 years, for your equity in it to double. That's a tough ask in today's property market, but it's not impossible.

Exponential growth

If you have *two* properties growing at 7.2 per cent, you've got two properties that are doubling in value in 10 years.

Let's say you buy a property for $600 000 and it doubles in value in 10 years so it's worth $1.2 million. Your equity is $600 000. Over those 10 years you might have paid down the loan a bit as well, making your equity even higher.

There's no way you'd save that much through normal savings over the same length of time. Even if you saved $20 000 a year, you'd only put away $200 000 over a decade. You'd have to triple those annual savings to make $600 000 in the same time.

If you were to *leverage* those properties, you could have three or four properties doing the same thing. In this way, you can create massive wealth from reasonably modest, achievable savings.

An average annual growth rate of approximately 7.2 per cent might sound high, especially as Australia's long-term annual growth average is at 6.4 per cent. But many suburbs across Australia have achieved and exceeded this growth rate over long periods.

This is particularly true of properties in high-demand, supply-constrained areas close to employment hubs, transport, schools and lifestyle amenities.

Let me show you what this looks like in practice with a simple example (see table 4.1). If you purchase a property today for $800 000 and it grows in value by an average of 7.2 per cent a year, in 10 years its dollar value will approximately double to around $1.6 million.

Table 4.1 *the value in compounding growth*

Year	Property value ($)
0	800 000
1	857 600
2	918 283
3	982 197
4	1 049 506
5	1 120 380
6	1 195 000
7	1 273 556
8	1 356 250
9	1 443 291
10	**1 534 905**

As you can see, the property's capital growth accelerates over time thanks to *compounding.*

In the first year it increases by a relatively modest $57 600. After that the value increases progressively because with each year that passes, the capital growth rate applies to an ever-larger value base. In the second year that 7.2 per cent applies to the property's increased value ($857 600) and so on in subsequent years. Over 10 years this compounding effect has resulted in your returns increasing *exponentially* to $1.6 million.

Capital growth is not a straight line

Here's where many investors trip up. They have their hearts set on doubling their money but while the target average annual growth rate might be 7.2 per cent, this doesn't mean the market will increase by that percentage every year. Some will grow at 4 per cent; others will boom for two years with double-digit returns then stagnate for five. Some will decline in value for a period. Typically, *property values move in cycles*, which means periods of rapid growth are followed by slowdowns or even declines.

This means the game isn't simply about owning property; the game is about owning the right properties in the right areas at the right times and *holding each through a complete market cycle.*

The same suburb may experience:

- 15 per cent growth in one year, during a market boom, followed by
- flat or declining growth of, say, negative 5 per cent during a market correction.

But across a 10-year period, the average annual growth in that suburb will be around 7 per cent.

I've seen this play out in my own portfolio. When I bought in Brisbane years ago, periods of explosive growth were followed by plateaus. The same happened with my properties in Sydney.

The key is not to panic during downturns or to become overconfident during booms. *The longer you hold a quality property in a growth area, the more short-term fluctuations will smooth themselves out and the more you will benefit from compounding.*

Time in the market is far more important than timing the market.

Due diligence for 7 per cent annual growth

Doubling your money in property within 10 years isn't a matter of luck. It's about following a proven strategy. To double your money in property in a decade, you want capital growth, compounding, leverage and momentum.

There are tried and tested strategies to achieve this goal:

- **Target owner-occupier demand.** Buy in areas where people want to live rather than in speculative hotspots. Look for areas with recent population growth. More people equals more demand equals upward pressure on prices. Focus on employment hubs and income growth. If an area attracts residents with higher incomes and more borrowing power, property values and rentals are likely to experience stronger growth. If wages rise, buyers can borrow and pay more. If wages stagnate, growth slows.
- **Follow government spending.** Government investment in infrastructure such as public transport links, hospitals, schools and employment hubs transforms local markets. It's a strong signal of long-term growth.
- **Look for areas with low stock levels.** If not much is for sale in the area where you're looking to buy, that's a good sign. High demand plus low supply equals strong competition, which pushes property prices up. Monitor rising rents. Rental pressure often signals future property price rises, improving property owners' cash flow.
- **Buy in locations with strong supply constraints.** Think beaches, regional hubs, island suburbs, clifftops, established leafy island and waterfront suburbs, pockets with no more land to release. Scarcity of available property in a desirable area multiplies growth in property values. Tight supply of land, limited development opportunities and zoning caps all drive upward price movement.

- **Buy at the right time in the market cycle.** You don't need to buy when the market in the area is at the very bottom of a cycle but avoid buying at the top of a boom. Leverage equity intelligently to accelerate growth as leveraging enables your returns to grow faster than your capital. You still invest safely but your money works harder. The increased equity can be used to purchase additional properties, further accelerating growth in your portfolio.
- **Use debt reduction to build equity.** Mortgage repayments, especially on principal-and-interest loans, reduce your debt on a property thereby increasing your equity in it.
- **Maximise tax benefits.** Depreciation, negative gearing and capital gains tax (CGT) discounts for properties held longer than 12 months can all enhance your return.
- **Revalue and recycle equity.** You buy, the property grows in value, you revalue it, pull out the equity and reinvest it. This is how smart investors double their money quickly, and double it again and again.

When all these elements align, doubling your equity in a property in just 10 years is achievable. But most investors look at only one of these growth-area markers—usually median price charts—and ignore the rest.

Locations where values have doubled in a decade

Many suburbs and regional areas across Australia have achieved average annual growth rates sufficient to enable properties to double in value over a decade. Here are some examples.

In New South Wales, suburbs such as Leppington in Sydney's south-west saw around 8 per cent annual growth over the decade from 2014 to 2024. That growth was driven by new infrastructure, including the extension of the Sydney Metro, and strong population growth.

In Victoria, Geelong achieved about 7.5 per cent annual growth over the same period, thanks to improved transport links together with affordability when compared to Melbourne.

Queensland's Sunshine Coast has seen around 7.8 per cent annual growth in the decade to 2024, driven by lifestyle migration and a limited supply of new land.

Western Australia experienced a marked downturn in property values for part of the same 10-year period, yet regional hubs such as Bunbury benefited from Perth's growth-ripple effect and from upgrades to local infrastructure to achieve around 7.3 per cent annual growth over the 10 years to 2024.

The examples in table 4.2 (overleaf) prove that doubling your money through property is possible across different market types: capital cities, lifestyle regions and regional areas with growing economies.

Be strategic and confident

Missing out on a quality investment property is rarely the result of bad luck. More often it comes down to a handful of very common mistakes, such as inexperience, lack of strategy, decision-making paralysis, emotional thinking, listening to the wrong people, obsessing over small price differences or simply moving too slowly. The good news? These errors can easily be avoided.

Table 4.2 *compound growth locations*

State/ Territory	Location	10-year growth rate % p.a. (approx.)	Comments
NSW	Leppington (Sydney's south-west)	8	Driven by new infrastructure, Sydney Metro extension and strong population growth.
Vic.	Geelong	7.5	Driven by a regional boom, improved transport links and the area's affordability compared to Melbourne.
QLD	Sunshine Coast	7.8	Rapid value increases driven by lifestyle migration and limited supply of new land.
WA	Bunbury	7.3	Benefited from Perth's 'growth ripple' effect and local infrastructure upgrades.
SA	Mount Barker	7.4	Driven by rapid regional development and by the area's affordability compared to the Adelaide metro area.
Tas.	Hobart	9	One of Australia's best performers over the decade, driven by strong population inflows and tight supply.
ACT	Belconnen	7.5	Steady growth supported by government employment stability and urban renewal projects.
NT	Darwin City	7.1	Growth has returned in recent years after cyclical lows earlier in the decade from 2014 to 2024.

Note: This data is based on CoreLogic and REA median-house-price growth trends from 2014 to 2024.

Too often a potential investor watches someone else buy the property they'd been cautiously considering and for a price they'd have been comfortable paying.

In a market like Australia's, decisiveness based on education and strategy is one of an investor's most powerful tools. When you're clear, confident and prepared, you won't need to hesitate, you won't overthink and *you won't miss out*. You'll secure high-performing properties that will meet your long-term strategy and compound your wealth in years to come.

To avoid missing out on great opportunities, you need to shift from reactive and emotional decision-making and become more strategic and confident.

Here are some big traps I often see.

Hesitation

One of the most common reasons investors miss out on great properties is simple: they just haven't been through the process enough times to understand *how quickly the market will move on a quality investment property*. Unfortunately, the market doesn't slow down to accommodate a novice buyer's learning curve.

Some investors delay moving forward on securing a property, despite its suitability, because they want another inspection or the opinion of family and friends, or they worry something better might show up. In a competitive market, hesitation costs the opportunity to buy the right property at the right time and reap the benefits.

It's also useful to understand how property moves at different speeds in different parts of the country and at different points in a market's cycle. Investors who are accustomed to slower markets often underestimate how quickly metropolitan and growth-area properties can transact.

Savvy Australian property buyers, particularly in high-demand investment markets such as Brisbane's north, Perth's growth corridors and Melbourne's middle-ring suburbs, rarely give inexperienced buyers time to 'think it over for a few days'.

A new investor often assumes they can take their time, revisit the property next weekend or spend a week researching comparable sales. An experienced investor has their due-diligence checklist ready to go and understands that delays can result in either losing the property or having to pay more for it.

The best properties won't wait.

So you need to become a buyer who can be decisive because they're well informed and prepared. If you're not ready, someone else will be.

No clear strategy

Many prospective property investors begin their journey without a clear strategy. They know they want to invest in property, but they don't know:

- what type of property suits their financial goals
- what yield they require
- what growth timeline they can expect
- what locations align with their risk profile
- what borrowing capacity they want to preserve for future purchases
- what their long-term portfolio structure should look like.

Without such a strategy, every property can look good or bad depending on your mood or other irrelevant factors. In reality, there is a buyer to suit every property, but not every property will suit every buyer.

Without a solid strategy based on knowing exactly what you want, you will be walking in blind. You risk being distracted by cosmetic details, minor imperfections and other features irrelevant to investment performance. You may think you have settled on finding a cash-flow-positive property, only to wonder whether what you're really after is blue-chip growth. Or is what you really want a development opportunity or a renovation project? So you hesitate, which leads to second-guessing, both of which waste time. Meanwhile, the market is moving.

Having a well-thought-out plan and a sound strategy will enable you to recognise what type of property and what location will best suit your risk profile. Even experienced investors often employ the services of experienced buyer's agents to help them execute property-investing strategies that align with their short- and long-term goals. An expert can help map out a clear path.

A well-thought-out property investment strategy acts as a filter. It helps you to recognise a great property deal instantly because it ticks all the boxes that align with your long-term goals.

Without a sound strategy, you risk floating from one bright idea to another, and you'll almost certainly risk overwhelm, indecision and missed opportunities.

Perfect property syndrome

New investors often fall into the trap of trying to find a property that has everything: high yield; high capital growth and low maintenance; a new build with development potential; a blue-chip location—all at a price under market value!

What I call Perfect Property Syndrome leads to decision paralysis. Its victims may dismiss great opportunities because they fail to distinguish the key fundamentals that are the drivers of long-term performance. Experienced investors know a good investment property doesn't need to be perfect. It just needs to meet your strategy.

Choking on the deal

As is normal with any risk-taking, even seasoned investors can hesitate to strike while the iron's hot. Risk-averse investors, however, may find the process so overwhelming that even when everything favours purchasing they simply can't decide.

Common fears include:

- paying too much
- choosing the wrong suburb
- interest rate rises
- potential damage by tenants
- negative cash flow.

What risk-averse investors must remember is that fear leads to hesitation, and hesitation kills deals.

While a potential investor's concerns may be valid, the risks I've listed are *manageable*—especially when mitigated by:

- due diligence
- solid research
- expert guidance
- an appropriate, stable financial buffer

- a well-thought-out investment strategy
- a dream team of expert advisers.

The investors who build long-term wealth are those who can make decisions based on data and knowledge and leave their emotions and anxiety aside.

Ironically, doing nothing is the biggest risk of all.

Don't sweat the small stuff

Some investors will fuss over $10 000 or $20 000 during negotiations. It's important not to sweat the small stuff and to always keep the bigger picture in mind. In reality, that extra $20 000 spread across a 30-year mortgage is negligible. More important, when that property's value grows by $200 000 over the next three to five years, as good properties in strong markets often do, that initial negotiation ceases to matter.

Smart investors understand that small price variations are insignificant in the context of long-term capital growth. The best property is rarely the cheapest; it's the one in the best location and the one that performs well, year in year out.

Poor advice

Well-meaning friends, parents, siblings and colleagues may feel compelled to offer property advice, especially when someone they know is about to make a big financial decision. But good intentions do not necessarily equate to good advice. It's important to recognise that family and friends may have:

- outdated views of the market
- limited experience
- a personal bias toward certain cities or suburbs

- a poor understanding of investment fundamentals
- an attachment to their own property experiences.

We've noted how an investor's fear can stop them from making a move on a good property, but a well-intentioned friend, colleague or loved one's opinions can work in a similar way. They might say:

- Oh, I wouldn't buy there.
- *That* seems expensive.
- Wait until the market cools.
- I heard interest rates might rise.
- My friend's cousin bought there and had a bad experience.

Experienced property strategists, buyer's agents and financial specialists operate according to hard data, sound research and current market conditions.

Emotional purchases

It's not a good idea to buy close to where you live, unless your strategy rather than your heart says it's the best investment location.

For a start, it has to have good capital growth potential. Some people live in very good suburbs where values don't increase much over time. But often properties in those suburbs cost more than most people want (or are able) to spend on an investment property anyway.

So you need to take the emotion out of it.

For example, I had a call from a new client in Darwin. I started off by talking about strategy and explaining that Aus Property Professionals are borderless, meaning that we like to look all over the country when we're ready to buy.

But this client told me he just wanted to buy in Darwin, because he lives there. That was interesting, because I think Darwin's property values have been artificially inflated by too much hype, with lots of buyer's agents buying for investors and pushing up prices.

I advised him Darwin was one of just two capital cities in Australia that had not achieved positive growth in the previous decade, but he was set on a property with good cash flow in the city. His aim was to buy several properties, one by one, each very close to where he lives so he could literally keep an eye on his investments.

I meet many people who think like this. 'I don't want to buy there; I want to buy a property close to where I live so I can check on it.' This makes no sense since under Australian law an owner is allowed to make a maximum of four inspections a year. You are not entitled to knock on the door and say, 'Hey, Joe Bloggs, this is my property; I just want to have a look through it.'

Buying poor assets

One of the biggest mistakes investors make is buying the wrong asset. They're often driven by marketing rather than by investment fundamentals. Off-the-plan apartments and house-and-land packages can look attractive because they're brand new and come with depreciation benefits, but you're usually paying a premium that includes the developer's margin. By the time the property settles it's not uncommon for the value to be the same as, or even below, what you paid.

The bigger issue is supply. Large apartment complexes and expanding outer estates can create ongoing competition that limits price growth and rental increases. Investment-grade property is about scarcity and strong owner-occupier demand. If endless similar stock is being built nearby, long-term performance is likely to suffer.

Run your property portfolio like a business

If you want your property portfolio to perform, run it like a business. In other words:

- **Build a clear strategy.** Keep in mind at all times your goals, your timeline, your preferred markets, your risk profile and your long-term plan. The investors who succeed are the ones who know what they're looking for.
- **Work with professionals.** Use experts who can guide you objectively because they know and understand the market. You'll almost certainly save your outlay on their services and often you'll gain a whole lot more.
- **Get educated.** Learn the fundamentals of growth, yield, supply/demand dynamics and portfolio structure. Know how to assess value.
- **Line up your financial ducks.** Have finance pre-approved. If you're clear on your budget, you'll be able to make calculated, informed and, when needed, rapid decisions.
- **See property purchases as business decisions.** Let the numbers lead your decisions and you'll avoid emotional pitfalls.
- **Move fast when a property fits your strategy.** Great opportunities won't wait. When the right one appears, be ready to move decisively.

Understand the long game

Doubling your money in property is not a get-rich-quick scheme—it's the culmination of strategic buying, patience and harnessing the power of compounding growth.

You don't need luck; you need a plan.

When property investors fail, it's usually because they buy emotionally or they buy into a market that's oversupplied or they fail to move strategically when the time is right.

The harsh truth is that most investors never double their money because they never build a plan that supports their goal. But with the right strategy and a long-term perspective, you can harness the power of compound growth to build real wealth.

Growth comes from increases in an area's population, residential income levels and infrastructure. These are coupled with supply constraints, which is to say demand exceeds supply. It follows that the most desirable properties are in areas that tick the boxes of strong demand, rising rents, low stock, wage growth and good infrastructure, or plans for major infrastructure projects. These advantages, coupled with leverage, equity, recycling and timing, enable the greatest compounding.

By targeting high-demand areas with strong fundamentals, such as good infrastructure, employment opportunities, lifestyle appeal and population growth, you can position yourself for long-term success. Because you are prepared you will be able take the right steps at the right time.

I'm passionate about helping everyday Australians to understand these principles. I've seen firsthand how transformative successful property investment can be — for building wealth and creating the freedom to spend time with your family and live life on your own terms.

What I can do is help you invest tactically, build momentum and stay ahead of the market. In the next chapters we can look together at property investment strategies that work.

Key takeaways

- The three keys to wealth creation through property are capital growth, leveraging debt and time in market.
- Capital growth accelerates over time thanks to compounding, leveraging your money to grow your income.
- Decisiveness based on education and strategy is one of the property investor's most powerful tools.
- Absence of a clear strategy, perfectionism, poor advice, emotion, hesitation, fear and anxiety, and buying poor assets are their biggest obstacles.

Chapter 5

Make planning and preparation a priority

Over the years I've helped close to 6000 clients buy property, from those stretched thin by mortgage stress to those who've structured their loans smartly and stayed in control. In this chapter I'll break down the role finance strategy plays in growing your property portfolio.

Why finance is crucial to building a portfolio

I've seen so many would-be investors' property dreams end before they begin because they haven't understood the key role finance plays. I don't want that to happen to you.

There's more to property investment than finding the right suburb, hunting down 'bargain' properties and being a killer negotiator. While those things are important, property investment is actually a game of finance. Being able to access other people's money in the form of bank loans is what enables you to make your first investment, and it's what allows you to keep buying.

I've seen many motivated would-be investors who have found the property they like, only to discover when they approach the bank that their borrowing capacity isn't what they'd thought. Or that the lender requires documents they can't quickly produce. Or that their broker hasn't structured things correctly. So the deal falls over.

Or worse, they have bought a property, only to learn that the way they've set up their loan makes a second purchase near-impossible.

This chapter isn't about how to get finance approved. It's about how to give finance its proper place in your strategy so you can build something substantial over time. It's about setting yourself up to *keep buying* rather than just buying once.

It's important to note you don't need to be a finance expert. That's what your mortgage broker is for. They help you deal with lenders, compare your options, figure out your borrowing capacity, and identify suitable strategies and schemes.

But even if you work with a mortgage broker, you do need to be aware of how the financing process works and what you need to do to be in the best position to use finance to your advantage.

Because it's so important, it's worth repeating: property investing is less a real estate game than a finance game. *Property is the vehicle, but finance is the fuel.* If there's no fuel, or if the fuel delivery system is faulty, it won't matter how good the vehicle is. It won't go anywhere.

This matters, because I'm guessing that like most potential investors, you don't want 50 properties. Your aim is not to become a billionaire. It is to reach a point where you're comfortable. You want options.

You want more time to enjoy life. You want security. You want to know your kids will be okay.

If you want those outcomes, you have to treat finance as a strategy rather than as a form you complete after the event.

A wish list is where property investment starts, not where it ends

When a new client comes to me, we usually begin with a written brief, or what I call a wish list. It's a starting point, a set of prompts that helps the client begin to articulate what they want not just from property investment but from life. Where do they want to be in 10 or 15 years? What are their passive-income goals? What are their retirement plans? The aim is not to lock them into a cage of rigid rules but to get the conversation moving. And it works really well.

Next comes a discovery meeting by phone or video link. I usually start by saying something like 'Thank you very much for filling out the wish list. Now let's embellish it. Talk to me a bit more about where you are in life, what your situation is, what you're trying to achieve.'

Because the wish list alone doesn't tell me enough, I dig deeper to tease out their goals and to form a bigger picture. It might tell me they want a property in a certain price range and with a certain yield. But it doesn't tell me what they want that property to do for them and their life.

In that conversation, I'm asking, 'Where are you now? And what are you looking to achieve in the next 15 years or so?'

Unless people are very specific and say, 'I just want to buy one property and that's it' or 'I just want to do a duplex', I always work backwards from their ultimate financial goal. That's the only way to build a strategy that makes sense.

Because *the most important thing is understanding your goals.* It's not just about buying that property. It's about understanding whether that property is going to fit your strategy and what you're trying to achieve.

If you don't do that important groundwork, you could end up with a property that doesn't actually move you closer towards the life you want. This is how you can get stuck. You buy one property... then drift.

Questions you need to ask

These are the questions that will help you shape a sound finance strategy. When I work with clients to start mapping out finance, we gather background information.

The first step in getting your finances together is to focus on what you're looking to achieve. There are some key things you'll have to think about so you know where you want to get to. Take some time and answer these questions for yourself.

Your goals and time frames

- What are your three main goals for investing in property?
- When would you like to buy? Is there a deadline?
- Do you have a passive income target? If so, what is it, and what is your time frame for achieving it?
- Do you have a capital growth or equity target? If so, how much is it, and what is your time frame for reaching it?

Your budget (excluding stamp duty and legal fees)

Your budget will be the amount you can raise from savings and loans to purchase property. At this stage, we will exclude stamp duty and legal fees. To help you grasp how much you actually want to invest, I'd ask you, as I ask my clients, to respond to these simple questions and list them from least to most relevant.

Is your budget determined by:

- your maximum borrowing potential
- the amount you are comfortable spending
- how much you think you'll *need* to spend
- wishful thinking
- other?

The deposit

- A 10 per cent deposit is usually required. Will you be using cash/savings or equity for that deposit?
- How much in cash/savings/equity do you have available for this purchase (your freedom fund)?

Finance

- Do you have a loan pre-approval? If so, please supply a copy of it.
- Do you have a mortgage broker or bank contact? If so, please supply their details.

Foreign investor requirements

- Do you have Australian citizenship or residency? If so, please provide evidence of this.
- Do you need Foreign Investment Review Board approval?

(continued)

Your existing property position

- Do you own other property/ies? If so, please supply the following:
  - Address
  - State
  - Property type (house, unit etc.)
  - Purchase date
  - Purchase price
  - Current estimated value
  - Weekly rent if applicable
  - Amount owing (debt).

Your home and family plans

- Do you currently own a family home? If so, is paying down the loan on it a priority? Is upgrading it a shorter-term goal? If you don't own your own home, is acquiring one a priority, or can it wait while you rent and put your money towards acquiring an investment property or properties?
- Do you have children, or are you planning a family?
- Is pursuing further education, starting your own business, a major lifestyle change or time on a single income part of your plan?

Your strategy preferences

- Is it more important for your property to be positively or negatively geared, and why? Positively geared means your investment pays you each month while negatively geared means it costs you money to hold.
- Have you sought advice around ownership structure? Will you be buying property in your own name(s) or purchasing

in a trust or self-managed super fund (SMSF)? What advice have you received so far?

- How do you feel about renovating property to add value? If you're prepared to renovate, what work, if any, would you do yourself?
- For how long do you plan to hold the property?
- Are you planning to live in this property at any stage?

These questions matter, because a finance strategy needs to apply to the person, the plan and the timeline.

Your goals drive your finance, not vice-versa

Once we have answers to all these questions, we can develop a strategy. We look at your goals, work out a strategy for achieving them and lay out some scenarios around them.

For example, if you're on a low income, buying the kind of high-priced properties with low yields found in Sydney is unlikely to be a viable option. A better strategy would be to seek properties in larger regional centres where higher yields are matched with strong growth.

We might conclude, for example, that:

- If $550 000 is your borrowing capacity, the first purchase should be in a region with strong growth, while you rentvest in Sydney.
- $550 a week is the yield you should target for your first property.
- You can increase equity and yield with a $20 000 renovation, so the property becomes positively geared.

- You'll need to get a revaluation and apply for refinancing to buy a second property on a large block.
- On the second property you'll build a granny flat and rent out both properties for dual income.
- You'll hold those properties and then sell them to buy a Sydney property, keeping the original property to help pay down your mortgage. This is how long it's likely to take.
- And this is what you'll need to do to ensure that your borrowing capacity is sufficient to enable you to follow the plan.

Similarly, if your plan is to buy four properties and sell two of them to pay off the other two within a 10-year period, you'll need to ensure you'll have enough borrowing capacity to do that. There's no point in buying one property that maxes out your budget and negatively impacts your ability to service a further loan (what lenders call your serviceability). It might seem like a great idea, but it will derail your plan before you begin.

That's why it's so important to start with the end in mind, only purchasing properties that will help you reach your goals in terms of equity and growth and that align with your finance strategy.

The position of an investor with $800 000 borrowing capacity is very different from that of an investor with $3 million borrowing capacity. If your capacity is lower, buying a property that produces cash flow will be important. Your strategy will be to look at high-yield, neutral to positively geared property, because that cash flow will help get you into another property sooner.

If you've got a higher borrowing capacity, you'll probably be okay with negative gearing because you're likely to be on a higher income. That income will mean you can service that first loan and be approved for further loans, enabling you to buy more properties and put together a positively geared portfolio.

Your written brief or wish list is just the beginning of your property search. Some things on your list will emerge as essential; others will diminish in importance. That's normal. What you don't want is to become so devoted to that first brief that you are reluctant to change in the face of new information.

Case study

Onto the property ladder at 25

Nathan came to me when he was 25 years old. At that age, I wasn't thinking about setting myself up for life financially — it was all about my music career. But young people today think differently. Nathan is a perfect example of that.

Limited borrowing capacity, but time on his side

Nathan works in IT, which has the potential to bring Nathan a high income, but he wasn't there at 25. He'd only been out of uni for a couple of years, and his borrowing capacity was about $600 000.

Here's the thing, though. Nathan had something more valuable than income: he had time. The strategy for a potential property investor in their twenties is completely different from that for someone in their fifties.

A younger investor has more time to wait for a property's capital growth to come through. Buying a high-growth, negatively geared property at 25 makes sense because you don't *need* a positive cash-flow property portfolio yet. That's what investors

(continued)

in their fifties, like my clients John and Rachel, have to consider. (I'll tell you about their strategy in chapter 9.)

At 25, you need to secure high-growth assets; you don't need to buy multiple properties in a year. If you begin investing at Nathan's age and you manage to buy another property every three or four years, you'll be setting yourself up really well.

The challenge: limited serviceability

With only $600 000 borrowing capacity, I couldn't devise a full, long-term strategy for Nathan yet, so my advice was that he buy the best growth asset he could afford. The most important thing was to get him onto the property ladder with a property with the potential for long-term capital growth.

Nathan wanted to get into what we call a rising market — a market about to take off. We also wanted to buy somewhere we could get decent cash flow — around 5 per cent — from his investment. Nathan wanted to look in regional NSW.

The search for a rising market

People often ask me, 'How do you know a rising market when you see one?' There will be increasing numbers of buyers in the market, prices will be beginning to increase and properties will be selling more quickly, so the number of days a property is on the market start to fall. And there's more FOMO around.

It's like catching a wave. Because you want to buy *before* a market booms, one that hasn't gone crazy yet. You look for the signs I listed earlier in this chapter.

The signs were all there in Orange, NSW, in 2025.

Orange is a solid regional city with good fundamentals. It's a university town with a growing population, it's about 3.5 hours from Sydney, so it benefits from the tree-change factor as people are priced out of the city or decide to downsize. There's a limited supply of land in the good areas and strong rental demand. The market in Orange was exhibiting strong rising-market indicators: more buyers, quicker sales, prices starting to move. But it hadn't boomed yet.

That's the sweet spot.

A similar thing has happened in capital cities such as Perth and Brisbane in recent years, though they weren't so much rising as *booming* markets.

The Orange property: within budget, long-term hold

We found Nathan a property in Orange that was within his budget at $575 000. We helped him find a tenant at $550 a week, for a 4.9 per cent gross yield. But this wasn't about getting immediate cash flow. It was about securing a growth asset that's going to compound over the next 20, 30, 40 years while he continues building his career and his income.

Fast-forward 12 months and the property was valued at $710 000 — more than $130 000 in capital growth in a year, without a hammer being lifted (see figure 5.1, overleaf). Shortly after his first property purchase Nathan got a new job, which came with a significant pay rise that enabled him to continue investing.

(continued)

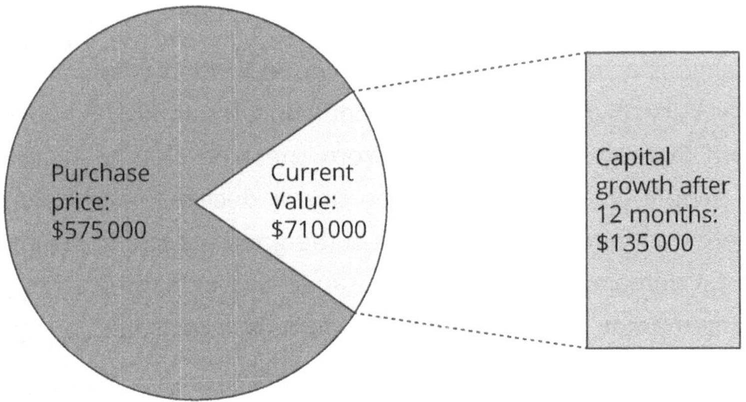

Figure 5.1 *Nathan's capital growth in just the first year*

Second time around, we decided to look at blue-chip markets and properties that would produce good, long-term capital growth, in accordance with Nathan's age and risk profile.

His next purchase would be in Melbourne. Why? Because Melbourne is historically the second-highest growth market in Australia after Sydney. However, its property market has gone flat in the past few years, following some of the Victorian Government's decisions around taxes on investors. Melbourne's property markets are now showing huge signs of recovery, and there are excellent opportunities to buy at good value before they really boom.

Nathan's long-term play

The beauty of beginning at 25 is time. A 25-year-old doesn't need to buy four properties in two years. An investor that age has the time to be patient, to buy quality and let compound growth do the heavy lifting. Here's how I see it playing out for Nathan.

He holds his Orange property, lets it grow in value, focuses on his career and increases his income. If his Orange property grows at just 7.2 per cent annually — which is pretty reasonable for a quality asset over the long term — this is what will happen:

- By the time Nathan is 35 the property will have doubled in value to $1.15 million.
- By the time he's 45 it will potentially have quadrupled to $2.3 million.
- When Nathan is 55 it will potentially be worth eight times what he paid for it, or $4.6 million.

These numbers might seem unbelievable, but if you had asked someone in 1975 whether the property they purchased then for $35 000 would be worth $1.5 million 50 years later, they might have said you were crazy. Once again, it's the magic of compounding we discussed in chapter 4.

In three or four years, with a higher income, Nathan might buy another property — by then he may be able to afford something better. Three or four years after that he might buy a third investment property. He won't need to rush.

At 35 he'll own multiple properties like Orange but across different markets. By the time he's 45 he'll have substantial equity in his freedom fund. At 55 he'll have a choice: keep working or transition to complete financial independence.

(continued)

Nathan's freedom fund strategy

- Start at age 25 as an IT worker with $600 000 borrowing capacity.
- Focus at first on long-term capital growth rather than cash flow.
- Buy in rising but not yet booming markets.
- Buy a quality property every three to four years and let time compound its value.

Note that starting young means extra decades of compound growth.

Nathan's advantage:

> Information + action = massive head start.

Why I'm careful about promises

I want to talk now about something most property advisers skip: accountability.

I don't want to be misleading. I don't promise my clients they'll get rich, though there are plenty of books out there that do that. The problem is, that sort of message can generate unrealistic expectations. It can also make people feel like they're failing if the path you've helped them lay out doesn't end up suiting them or their lifestyle.

I'm especially careful when I discuss strategies because I think of clients in their thirties, forties and fifties and what's worked for them and what hasn't. And usually what *hasn't* worked is not the strategy we devised—it's the budget, the income or the attitude.

I've seen people fill out their wish list and do the introductory call, and they're excited. But they'll buy one property and stop. They don't stick to the plan. They simply don't want to buy that second investment property.

Or they stop working, then wonder why they can't move forward on their strategy. There are people who read *Positively Geared* and misunderstand the lessons. They'll say, 'I want to do what you did. *You* quit your job when you bought property—I want to do that too.' So they buy one property and quit working. But hang on; that's *not* what I did. I was buying properties for 10 or 15 years before I quit my teaching job. I didn't just buy one and stop working, expecting that one property to buy me financial freedom.

I've even known people quit their jobs *before* they buy their first property. They'll say, 'I've got the finance in place—but I just quit my job. Can I buy this property within three months so the banks don't have to see another pay slip?'

Accountability matters.

You're not going to achieve your goals just because you wrote them down. You will achieve them by continuing to work towards them and by staying in a position that will allow you to execute your plan.

Finance is a huge part of that. The moment your income disappears, your borrowing capacity shrinks. Your options are reduced and your momentum slows—or stops altogether.

So yes, we talk about interest rates and lenders. We also stress that you need to stay accountable to the plan, because the plan only works if you keep doing the work.

Borrowing capacity and credit

One good rule of thumb is that a bank will typically lend you around five to seven times your income. And you've probably heard this rule: *Don't spend more than 30 per cent of your pre-tax income on your mortgage.* This applies to your principal place of residence (PPR) when you're the one paying your mortgage. It doesn't apply to investment properties since your tenants' rent essentially helps you to pay down the mortgage on the property they're renting. But these figures are only a rough starting point, and can be misleading depending on your circumstances.

One reason people get caught out when paying off property loans is that they assume serviceability is simple. I earn *x*; I spend *y*; I can borrow the difference. But that's not how banks assess loan eligibility.

Banks use *assessment rates*, not actual interest rates. They build in buffers, often around 3 per cent above the current interest rate. So even if you're paying 6 per cent interest, the bank might assess you at 9 per cent. The idea is to stress-test you. They want to know you will still be able to service the loan should rates rise by three percentage points.

Lenders also use living expenses benchmarks to assess your capacity to service a loan. Even if you tell them you can live on almost nothing, they'll compare your declared expenses to standard measures such as the *household expenditure measure* (HEM). If your declared expenses are too low, the bank will ignore them in favour of their benchmark.

Then there's *existing debt*. This includes the obvious things like personal loans and car loans, but also HECS and credit-card debt, and buy now–pay later facilities. Even if you pay your credit card off fully each month, banks don't count that in your favour: it's the card's overall limit that matters. Banks assess your liability based on the card limit rather than the balance because you could draw that money down at any time.

This means that if you have a credit card with a $10 000 limit, the bank will assess you as though you had maxed out that card, thus reducing your borrowing capacity.

And if you already own investment property, banks usually 'shade' the rental income. Often they'll count only around 70 per cent of the rent you receive. They assume you may not get the other 30 per cent thanks to vacancies and property-related expenses. So your cash flow might be fine, but your assessed income from that property will be substantially lower than what you actually receive.

Put all this together and you can see why online calculators can be misleading. They simply don't capture the way lenders assess your capacity to pay down a loan.

This is one reason why you need to get your finance ducks in a row early in the process rather than after you've committed to buying.

Credit profile: small things matter

The next factor to consider is credit. A lot of investors don't realise how much small credit issues can change lender options. Having issues with credit might not stop you borrowing, but it can reduce the pool of lenders who'll approve you and that can influence your rates, terms and ability to keep buying.

Credit scores and comprehensive credit reporting have become far more influential in Australia. Lenders look at your repayment history, your credit utilisation and the pattern of your loan applications.

One of the most common mistakes people make is creating unnecessary credit enquiries before applying for a major loan. They switch providers, apply for new cards to get additional points, take out small finance products or let multiple brokers run multiple applications. This is not good practice as each enquiry can have a negative effect on your credit rating, potentially leading to lenders refusing to approve your loan.

Another thing people fail to factor in is that credit limits matter. Managing limits on your credit cards can improve your borrowing capacity, even if all those cards are paid off monthly. Again, the lender looks at your maximum potential exposure to financial risk rather than what you owe today.

If there are errors in your credit report, fix them ahead of time. Don't wait until you have a loan application in progress, because a credit issue could cost you vital negotiating power and time.

Choose the right lending structure

Once you understand the importance of both borrowing capacity and a deposit strategy, the next issue is deciding on the best lending structure. The structure you choose matters because your first loan doesn't just get you into the first property; it sets the tone for your entire portfolio.

First you have the choice of a fixed or a variable loan. Fixed means you have a locked-in interest rate for a set period, typically two to five years. A variable loan changes as interest rates change.

Then you need to decide between an interest-only loan or one where you pay off principal and interest. Do you want a loan split to create flexibility? You will discuss this with your mortgage broker, but you might also bring it up with your buyer's agent.

If you choose an interest-only loan, for example, your repayments might be lower, which frees up your borrowing capacity so you can buy another property sooner rather than later, but you're not increasing your equity by paying down the loan.

Then there's the decision to pay down the loan through an offset account or a redraw facility. An offset account reduces the interest you pay while keeping your savings accessible, whereas a redraw facility lets you pull back extra repayments you've already made, helping lower interest while still providing some flexibility if you need the funds later.

A lot of investors want simple answers here, like 'Always choose a fixed-interest loan' or 'Always opt for an interest-only loan'. But finance doesn't work like that. Which is better for you depends on interest-rate cycles, your risk tolerance, the size of your cash buffer and what you plan to do next.

One of the most important distinctions I make with clients is between deductible and non-deductible debt. If you're buying a principal place of residence, I generally recommend that you pay that mortgage down as fast as you can because it's non-tax-deductible debt.

Investment property debt won't necessarily be the first loan you pay down. Sometimes you need to leverage that; maybe instead of fast-tracking repayments that are tax-deductible, use the equity you've gained in that property to buy another. So paying investment debt down is not always the priority. Usually, the priority is controlling your risk while preserving your ability to keep buying.

This is where structures like offsets can be powerful, because they let you reduce interest without permanently locking money away. And loan splits can help, because they give you options later. A split loan divides your home loan into two or more parts, allowing you to combine fixed and variable interest rates to balance stability with flexibility. You can choose the proportion—for example, 50 per cent fixed, 50 per cent variable—to hedge against rate rises while still benefiting from potential rate drops or using offset accounts.

I'm not giving tax advice here, but I will say this: ownership structure and lending structure should be thought about together. Seek expert advice around whether to buy in your own name(s), or through a trust or company structure or self-managed super fund (SMSF), because that choice affects lending, borrowing and long-term flexibility.

Diversify lenders: why use multiple banks?

This is one of the biggest practical factors in portfolio growth. If you have all your loans with one lender, that lender will end up 'owning you', in a sense. They'll restrict how much you can borrow over time because to them you'll seem too exposed. And when other lenders see that, they mightn't lend to you either, because they'll see you as 'concentrated risk'.

Diversifying means using different banks as well as different lending structures. That includes fixed and variable interest mixes, interest-only and principal-and-interest loans, and so on.

There's also just the simple reality that multiple lenders helps you keep your options open.

Let me give you a real-life example. I had a young couple come to me recently. They were maxed out: they had two loans, both with ANZ, and they'd hit the wall. They wanted to build a portfolio but had only about $100 000 left in borrowing capacity. They said their broker couldn't get them any more money.

They also had money in an SMSF, and interestingly the bank *would* lend them around $700 000 if they chose that pathway. So there was a route forward, but the bigger issue was that their broker hadn't even tried other lenders. It sounded as though the broker was affiliated with ANZ in some way. When I asked them whether they had approached other lenders, they said no.

I suggested they look at other lender options including second-tier lenders, because they often have different serviceability calculators and may lend when major banks won't. Second-tier lenders offer home loans and financial products without holding the full banking licences of 'Big Four' banks. They include smaller banks, building societies, credit unions and non-bank lenders. They offer more flexible lending criteria for self-employed, bad credit, or lower-deposit borrowers, often at slightly higher rates.

Some of them are owned or backed by the majors anyway. The point isn't to go non-bank. The point is to *match your choice of lender to your strategy.*

This couple's broker was a friend who lived up the street and 'knew the area'. But they weren't planning to buy there anyway. And knowing local streets doesn't help if the broker can't structure finance to keep you moving. I referred them to a broker who *could* diversify their lender strategy because that's how I built my portfolio.

Once one major bank stopped lending to me, I went to a second-tier lender and a third-tier lender. That's how you grow. Not by staying loyal to one bank.

Have your documentation ready: the speed advantage

Prepared borrowers move faster—and speed matters. There are markets in which good properties don't sit around waiting for you to organise pay slips and bank statements. If you're slow, a better-prepared buyer will swoop in.

So part of getting your ducks in a row is doing boring stuff like getting your documents together. This is something you will need to do so your mortgage broker has all the relevant information at the ready.

One of the first considerations is whether you are a PAYG employee or self-employed. The borrowing process for PAYG applicants is generally straightforward, with many lenders only requiring two pay slips.

Self-employed borrowers may need to show tax returns, financials and up-to-date documentation that reflects the real performance of their business. Lenders often want the Notice of Assessment for the most recent financial year completed, and they may average your income(s) across a number of years.

If you already have investment properties, you'll need to produce any existing loan documents, as well as rental statements. And before you apply for a loan you'll need to have a clear understanding of what constitutes living expenses. In other words, you need to be organised.

This is another reason the finance conversation must happen early. It gives you time to clean things up and get your documentation and financial records together and avoid risking the timely approval of your loan application.

Who you'll need on your dream team

Many people don't realise it's about more than finding a good mortgage broker. It's about surrounding yourself with a whole team of experienced people you trust. As well as a broker, you'll need a buyer's agent, an accountant and a solicitor/conveyancer.

Buyer's agent

A buyer's agent will source property that meets your criteria and then negotiate to ensure you purchase the right property at the right price and, more important, on the right terms. They will walk you through the property investment process from start to finish.

They will set your strategy, provide research on recommended markets, source properties in line with your strategy, and provide full due diligence and property reports. Your buyer's agent will also assist in facilitating the signing of the contracts, work with your mortgage broker to get finance over the line, and organise building and pest inspections. Your buyer's agent will also undertake inspections and organise a property manager to acquire tenants.

Mortgage broker

If you go straight to a bank, you're unlikely to get the best deal. A mortgage broker has access to multiple lenders and will help you to find the loan best suited to your needs. They will get to know your individual circumstances and work hard to find the best finance solution for you. They'll help you set short-term and long-term finance goals that ensure you can enact your property strategy.

Brokers dominate the Australian market for a reason. A good broker doesn't just submit an application; they model scenarios, understand policy nuances and map borrowing capacity across lenders. They think about how your first purchase will affect your second.

They also help reduce the risk of failed applications, which matters because being declined for a loan can hurt your credit profile and make future approvals harder.

A broker can also give you an idea of how much you might be able to borrow, and the odds of your loan application being approved.

Accountant

Your accountant will advise you on buying a property that aligns with your circumstances. For example, should you purchase it in your own name or through a trust, company or other entity? Getting the purchasing structure right can be crucial when you're building a property portfolio, not least because of tax consequences.

Solicitor/conveyancer

Your solicitor will facilitate any relevant contracts. They will review documents and ensure that everything in any contract you sign is as it should be. They can also negotiate any changes to a contract. A solicitor is a qualified lawyer who can provide legal advice as well as handle property transactions, while a conveyancer specialises specifically in managing the legal paperwork involved in buying and selling property.

Others on your dream team

You'll also need a building and pest inspector, to ensure there are no nasties lurking under the surface of the property, and an insurance broker to help with a depreciation schedule for tax purposes. If you're buying a house to live in, they can help with an insurer for home and contents, or building and landlord's insurance if you're buying an investment property.

How to find your team

Referrals and word-of-mouth are really important—you'll need people who come highly recommended. Remember they don't need to be in the same physical location as you or even in the city or region you're buying into. (An exception to this rule is your building and pest inspector of course, because they'll need to access the property to carry out their work.) They just need to hold a valid licence to operate in that area.

You don't need to find a new team when you purchase in a new location. Once you have found the right team, use them for every deal you do.

A good team is just that. A team you can trust, whose members work together cohesively, communicating well and often, will give you a solid advantage over the average mum-and-dad investor who's likely to be less sure of what they are doing and why.

Everyone on your dream team must be strategically aligned and working towards your end goal, and to this end it's important they all understand what you're trying to achieve. It will keep you on track, too, when everyone works together in your best interests.

It isn't just about each individual transaction; it's about attaining your long-term goal.

To find your dream team, do your research before thinking seriously about who you'll engage. As goes for anything you're trying to achieve in life, it's important that you align yourself with people who have been there and done that, who have actually achieved what you want to achieve.

Ideally, you'll have your dream team for the long term, and they'll keep you on track with your strategy and remind you of *why* you're doing what you're doing.

Once I found my team, I became much more efficient at building my property portfolio and wealth. Because the process was streamlined, much of the stress was gone. All I had to do was send my team an email saying I was purchasing another property and everyone would swing into action.

Having a good team of professionals at the ready means when a really great property becomes available, you'll have the advantage of being able to move really quickly.

Understand what you buy

I firmly believe you should understand fully any asset you are buying. I tell my clients, don't invest until you understand what you're investing in. Sometimes clients say, 'Whatever you reckon—I trust you.' My response is, 'Don't trust *me*; trust the research and trust the data. Understand what I'm suggesting.'

The same principle applies to finance. Don't take out a loan you don't understand. Don't rely on an adviser's reassurance without getting a second opinion. *Ask questions until everything makes sense to you,* because a problem with outsourcing everything is that you can end up in trouble if you don't understand the risks.

Prepared investors keep moving

If you're serious about building a portfolio, getting your ducks in a row financially is the most important first step. It's also the difference between buying a property and hoping for the best and buying with a plan that enables you to continue to move.

One of the saddest patterns I see is when people buy one property and then unintentionally cap their portfolio growth. This can happen for a number of reasons.

They might cross-collateralise—which means two or more properties secure a single loan—without understanding the consequences. (Cross-collateralising poses significant risks, primarily allowing lenders to seize multiple assets if you default on one loan. It ties your properties together, making it difficult to sell or refinance individual assets without lender approval. It also reduces equity control, restricts lender options and often leads to higher, more complex fees.)

They might max out their borrowing capacity on their first property purchase, without a plan to guide them on what would best suit their goals. Or they choose a lender based on the offered interest rate alone. Two years later they wonder, 'Why can't I buy again?'

Finance needs to be designed with the *next* purchase in mind. If there's one thing I want you to take from this chapter, it's this: *the property you buy matters, but the finance strategy behind it matters more, because it determines what you can do next.*

The good news is that *you* don't need to be an expert on finance. That's what a good mortgage broker is for. But to help your broker devise the best finance strategy for you, you need to know the right questions to ask.

It's also your responsibility to get your personal finances in place and to get organised by acquiring key information and compiling relevant documentation. That way, when you start talking to a mortgage broker, you'll be ready to go. Now let's work out where to buy.

Key takeaways

By working through the following simple checklist you'll avoid the mistakes that prevent investors from growing their portfolios past that first property purchase:

- Get your finance ready early. Don't wait until you've found the property.
- Build your dream team: do your research to find an experienced, trustworthy team of buyer's agent, mortgage broker, accountant and solicitor/conveyancer.
- Understand your real borrowing capacity; don't rely on a calculator estimate.
- Clean up your credit: reduce limits where appropriate and avoid unnecessary enquiries.
- Document everything, including pay slips, tax returns, loan statements, rental statements and expenses.
- Build buffers: be prepared to put some cash in an offset account after you've purchased the property. Stress-test rate rises by seeing whether your budget could handle higher interest rates. If you couldn't handle a few hundred dollars a month more, you may be stretched too far and will need to build up a cash buffer. The lenders have what is called an assessment rate where they will assess a loan application at a rate of 3 per cent higher than the interest rate they will offer you. This is to ensure you will be able to afford repayments if rates rise. This is the bank's own stress test.
- Plan your next purchase: look into lender diversification and how you can create flexibility. Avoid cross-collateralisation.
- Do your due diligence — don't buy what you don't understand.

Chapter 6

Identify what property to buy and where

People are crazy about property in Australia. It makes sense given its history of massive growth and wealth creation, particularly over the past 50-odd years. So I recommend you get on board and give it a go.

Australian real estate is a good investment, but it's also pretty pricey by global standards. Let's dig into why this is, and what it means for you as an investor or homeowner.

Over the years I've guided thousands of clients through their property journeys and I've witnessed just how wide the gap has grown between property prices and household incomes. So let's break down how you might look at where to buy, whether you're after growth or yield or a balance of both for the long term.

How Australian housing affordability compares globally

If you've ever felt your eyes water at an Australian auction, you're not alone. Across several credible benchmarks, Australia stands out as one of the world's most expensive places to buy a home. One recent global comparison of 60 countries ranked Australia sixth for the price of a 'typical' apartment purchase per 100 m^2, behind Norway, Austria, Luxembourg, South Korea, and—most expensive—Switzerland.

We know property prices down under are high by world standards, but how affordable is property for average Australians? To assess that, we need to look at both *property values* and *average incomes*.

According to the Australian Bureau of Statistics (ABS), average annual earnings for a fulltime adult employee in May 2025 was $104 520. The mean dwelling price nationwide reached about $1 million in the March quarter of 2025 (though this varied significantly from state to state or territory).

That gap—between what a typical full-time worker earns and what a typical home costs—especially in the large cities where most of us live—is what makes experts refer to a property market as expensive.

But though the cost of a dwelling in Australia may seem prohibitive, average citizens in many other countries have an even more difficult time getting onto the property ladder. Take South Korea. Property prices in the Republic of (South) Korea are the world's second-highest, but the average full-time worker there earned just AU$48 906 in 2025.

In Switzerland it's a different story. The OECD estimated that full-time Swiss employees earned an average of AU$119 726 in 2024.

So even though property there costs a bundle, most working Swiss adults can afford it.

Norway's housing prices rank fifth in the world, just above Australia's, and Norwegians also enjoy high incomes by global standards: the average employed adult there earns a healthy AU$105 437 a year.

To put it into perspective, Australians earn just a little less than their Norwegian and Swiss counterparts, at $104 520, but more than twice as much as South Koreans, and all three countries have higher median dwelling prices than Australia does.

While property is expensive, it doesn't mean you can't buy a home. You might just have to think strategically. We will cover strategies in chapters 7 to 9.

Why is Australian property so pricey?

There's no single culprit — it's a mix of factors:

1. **Demand exceeds supply in areas deemed desirable.** One of the most important factors driving property prices up is limited supply in desirable areas. Most Australians live in a handful of capital cities and strict planning controls mean new land releases are limited. Because demand is concentrated in high-amenity zones, prices there rise.
2. **Population growth and migration increase demand.** Australia continues to attract new residents, international students and skilled migrants. That consistent inflow keeps both rental and buyer demand strong, especially in metro hubs.

3. **There are issues constraining construction.** Construction bottlenecks, labour shortages, higher material costs **and** slow approvals have restricted delivery of new housing across Australia. The National Housing Finance and Investment Corporation (NHFIC) has warned that supply continues to lag well behind demand.
4. **There are tax and finance hurdles.** Policies such as negative gearing, capital gains tax (CGT) discounts and investor-friendly lending keep money flowing into the property sector, further inflating values.

All these factors combine to create a market that's not only competitive but is increasingly difficult for first-home buyers to break into.

Transparent, low-risk markets with financial and tax incentives

For domestic investors, being able to tax-deduct interest paid on your mortgage against rental income (negative gearing) and the capital gains tax discount have long shaped incentives.

Why global investors favour Australian property

Despite high entry prices, Australia ticks a lot of the boxes for international investors:

- **Economic and policy stability.** Australia has a strong and mature banking system alongside strong laws and policies governing our economic sector.
- **Lifestyle and livability.** Sydney, Melbourne, Adelaide and Perth consistently rank near the top of global livability indices, and this supports steady demand for both owner-occupier and rental housing.

- **Population growth.** Australia is a popular choice for international migrants. These include international students and temporary workers who create a tight rental market, particularly in inner-city and middle-ring unit precincts and in suburbs close to universities and teaching hospitals.
- **Strong yields.** While yields—rental returns—on Sydney houses are slim, those in some other cities and specific regional markets are more attractive. Generally yields on townhouses and apartments are more attractive for investors; in some capital cities, apartment yields can be very favourable. Property of all types in go-ahead regional centres with growth drivers can also provide great yields and cash flow for foreign investors.
- **Scalable markets.** The recovery of Perth and Brisbane markets has reminded investors that Australia is not a one-city story. Diversifying your properties, and hence your exposure to risk across cities and product types, is a smart move.

Setting up your life strategy

What does all this mean if you're looking to invest? When prices are high, smart investors succeed not by *outspending* others but by *outstrategising* them:

- **Be realistic about entry costs.** You are competing with global capital and local demand.
- **Avoid emotion.** For example, prestige doesn't always equal performance.
- **Focus on fundamentals.** Think location, infrastructure, schools, local jobs growth, 'lifestyle' appeal.

(continued)

- **Look beyond big cities.** Emerging regional and outer metropolitan areas can deliver equally good growth and yield.
- **Understand supply pipelines, future zoning and construction trends.** These can change everything.
- **Diversify your portfolio.** Spread your investment risk across cities, price brackets and property types.
- **Don't chase hot spots.** When it comes to buying property in Australia, location is everything. Don't just follow the crowd or chase the latest hot spot — do your research and understand what's really driving the market.

Where are the most expensive properties (and why)?

It's important to recognise that affordable properties are not spread evenly across the country. Sydney median property prices are sky-high; Darwin's are less than half Sydney's. Other state and territory capitals have median combined house-and-unit prices ranging between the high $700 000s and upwards of $1 million.

There are good opportunities out there from coast to coast. In January 2026 the property platform Domain forecast that all Australian capital cities except Darwin would crack the $1 million price median in 2026.

Note that while median property values move monthly, the ranking across Australia's capital cities is pretty consistent.

The country's priciest properties are concentrated in prestige, amenity-rich enclaves with natural constraints on new supply.

So Australia's most expensive property markets are in Sydney's eastern suburbs and harbourfront (Point Piper, Vaucluse, Bellevue Hill), the Lower North Shore and select Northern Beaches; in Melbourne it's Toorak, Brighton and South Yarra and in Brisbane it's the inner-east riverfront.

These suburbs attract the wealthiest buyers with a winning combination of blue-chip school catchments, protected view corridors, and scarce prime land. And a deep buyer pool—both local and international—keeps the market buoyant. Sydney's high-end properties offer a lifestyle among the rich and famous alongside priceless Sydney landmarks such as the Harbour Bridge and Opera House and/or water views and beach access. Supply is limited and everybody wants to buy there.

Where are the cheapest homes (and why)?

At the other end of the spectrum, affordability is concentrated in the smaller capitals and the growing regional towns. Darwin's property market sits in a very different position compared to Sydney, Melbourne or Brisbane.

It consistently posts the lowest median value of any Australian capital city. This reflects its comparatively small economy, lack of job opportunities and the consequent lower average socio-economic status of its population and its larger proportion of lower-density homes. PropTrack and other real-estate trackers repeatedly flagged Darwin's median at around the low-to-mid $500 000s across 2024–25.

Darwin's smaller population (approximately 150 000 in the urban area) means the buyer pool is small. Less competition means lower property prices. Further, the city's tropical climate—hot and humid with monsoonal rains—discourages investors, as does its geographical distance from other Australian cities.

Darwin's economy is quite volatile because it is heavily linked to defence, government services, mining and infrastructure projects. Many residents are not permanent; they're Fly In, Fly Out (FIFO) workers. Fewer long-term residents can make it harder for landlords to find and retain good tenants.

While yields from Darwin property can look attractive, the city's capital growth has historically been both weaker and more volatile than that of other Australian cities. If you're looking for an affordable investment property, what you can learn from Darwin's historical property price movements is to look for cheaper properties elsewhere that have all the 'investment-grade markers' Darwin lacks.

If buying rurally, look for jobs growth and good job opportunities, a comfortable climate, an economy that doesn't rely on limited industries and, of course, a growing population.

Understand market cycles: the Perth peak

In terms of market cycles, Perth has been one of the most interesting markets to watch in recent years. After a prolonged downturn, in 2024 it became the hottest property market in the country. House prices jumped 24.2 per cent, units climbed 21.4 per cent and median values surged to $745 000 by December, from $564 700 at the end of 2023. Migration was booming and supply couldn't keep up. By early 2025 Perth looked unstoppable, and investors flooded in.

But then growth began to moderate. By mid 2025 dwelling values were up 8.6 per cent year-on-year—still healthy, but well down from their double-digit highs. The Real Estate Institute of WA was forecasting house price growth of just 5 to 10 per cent for 2026.

On the property clock, it appears that by the end of 2025 Perth was nearing 12 o'clock—the peak of its cycle—which often signals a coming plateau. However, Western Australia was forecast to build just 16 800 homes in 2025, while the population was expected to grow by 90 000. This massive housing supply shortfall means upward pressure on prices is continuing.

This example of the way markets move in cycles shows why understanding the fundamentals behind growth is important.

I like to go where the research and the data are pointing. I look at things like infrastructure, population growth, jobs growth and markets—as well as at things like how much the government is investing in a market.

Capital cities vs regional towns

Don't overlook regional Australia. There are many large regional cities that perform very well and also offer high yields. But there are pros and cons:

- **Population inflows from capital cities.** Since the COVID-19 pandemic Sydney and Melbourne residents have continued to move outward, chasing affordability and lifestyle—though this is shifting as employers bring staff back in-house and as tree-changers realise they don't like country life as much as they thought they would.

- **Regional infrastructure upgrades.** Fuelling the move to regional hot spots are infrastructure upgrades—highways, railway line extensions, hospitals, schools. In recent years, government spending has exploded in key regions.
- **Strong rental pressure.** Vacancy rates in many regional towns across Australia are lower than those in the big cities. In some cases, they are sitting below 1 per cent.
- **Higher relative yields.** Investors can achieve stronger cash flow in regional markets than in metropolitan markets without sacrificing growth—if they pick the right town.
- **Employment decentralisation.** This has helped many regional towns and cities move ahead in recent years, as new business parks, distribution centres, hospitals and education hubs have spread economic activity along regional corridors. The result is a demand base that's booming and a market that is both more stable and more diversified.

The downside: buying in the wrong town

Be aware that not every regional town is a good investment. In fact, most aren't. Here's where those investing in regional property can get caught out.

- **Risk 1:** Single-industry towns. If a regional city or town relies on just one employer or one industry, whether it's mining or agriculture or a specific manufacturing plant, local property investment risk skyrockets. I've invested in such an environment, and it's not a good thing.

- **Risk 2:** No long-term population growth. If people aren't actually moving to a particular town or region, the property market there won't grow.
- **Risk 3:** An oversupply of new housing. Large estate releases can drown a local market in new stock, killing capital growth.
- **Risk 4:** Thin markets. Some regional towns have such low sales volumes that prices can stagnate or become volatile.
- **Risk 5:** No economic depth. As a property investor, you're looking for towns with job opportunities in multiple sectors, not those with fragile economies.

The rise of lifestyle

What makes a property appealing is the same as what makes them grow in value—pleasant quiet streets and proximity to shopping strips and public transport, good schools and universities. None of this has changed but property buyers' priorities have shifted somewhat since the COVID-19 pandemic, which caused many of us re-evaluate our priorities. Work–life balance and lifestyle factors have taken a front seat as drivers of growth in property value.

Lately I've bought properties for clients in locations that have growth drivers that are very different from traditional ones. As people increasingly value quality of life and work–life balance, they want to be close to the beach or to nature, or both. And locations that allow this—particularly beachside locations—are achieving massive growth.

Our family holiday home at Mollymook on the NSW South Coast is a good example of this. There are no schools, no university and the nearest doctor is in the next town, so people buy there primarily for lifestyle.

The bottom line is that nowadays more people are looking for lifestyle upgrades. They want to buy, for example, close to white-sand beaches. They want a holiday home far, but not too far, from the city. There's so much demand for houses that tick these lifestyle boxes that Mollymook property prices continue to soar. Today, prices for places near the beach can match those of some of the pricier eastern and northern suburbs of Sydney.

The Hemsworth effect

Speaking of growth cycles, here's an interesting case study that illustrates how markets can move.

While many regional areas grew substantially in value during and after the COVID-19 pandemic, Byron Bay on NSW's northern coast saw unprecedented growth.

Byron has always been a bit of an anomaly when it comes to regional property values because of its popularity with sea-changing Sydneysiders, its beachside location and the many local drawcards for those seeking a relaxed alternative lifestyle.

But at the start of the 2020s, actor Chris Hemsworth moved back there. Suddenly the town was drawing A-list interest from all over the world, especially from Hollywood. Zac Efron rented a $22 million mansion nearby in 2020 before purchasing a 128-hectare estate north of Byron for $2 million. Matt Damon stayed in a European-style mansion during the filming of *Thor: Love and Thunder*.

This period saw median house prices climb to an extraordinary $3.45 million by June 2022. I was quoted in the media as saying that the presence of celebrities was a 'major factor for Byron Bay'.

Then, in one year, prices plummeted by 31.3 per cent to just $2.3 million, leaving the median house price there just 7 per cent higher now than it had been at the end of 2020. (For context, house prices in Brisbane, Perth and Adelaide almost doubled over the same period, while prices elsewhere in regional NSW climbed by about 48 per cent.)

Of all property locations in Australia, Byron Bay experienced one of the worst declines in house prices in recent years. Why? Because houses were way *over*valued for property in what is, essentially, a smallish coastal town lacking traditional growth drivers. That's my take on it anyway.

Beware of unsustainable growth

A property price of $10 million in a sleepy town like Mollymook seems high, but $22 million in Byron Bay is ridiculous. The bottom line is they're just not worth that much! So no-one's going to *pay* that much once the excitement has worn off.

People wanted to be part of a community that attracted all these celebrities. Unfortunately for those who'd invested during the boom part of that cycle, the Hemsworth effect created *unsustainable growth*. In the end, Byron Bay—for better and worse—is still just a small coastal town.

That's not to say some of my clients who bought in the region—not in Byron Bay, but in nearby Lennox Head and with duplex developments there—didn't do really well. Those clients made heaps of money. It was lucky. I picked the right market, at the right time.

Still, there are very few traditional growth drivers in small coastal towns. Value there is all about lifestyle factors.

Once the short-lived celebrity bubble ceased to drive property price growth in Byron, other growth factors, such as good transport, community and educational infrastructure, population increases and jobs growth, didn't really stack up, so property values fell.

This is a perfect example of how markets don't move in straight lines and why understanding the fundamentals behind growth is so important.

Will Australian property always be expensive?

Are Australian property values ever likely to go down significantly?

The general answer is 'No—they're never going to go down'!

Nothing in housing is permanent, but several forces are hard to unwind. The concentration of coastal demand, planning frictions, construction constraints and continued international migration mean Australia is likely to remain expensive on a global scale. So if you're reading this book hoping that if you sit on the sidelines, property will be cheaper in a few years, you're wrong. That's not going to happen.

What you need to focus on is buying what you can afford, because there *are* still affordable Australian properties in some regions. There are occasionally going to be price declines in certain areas—places like western Sydney or western Brisbane where there are too many investors. Mining towns, too, experience property crashes every now and again.

Properties in places where people want to live (the 'good' parts of capital cities, strong regional locations, properties near the coast) rarely or never go backwards in value. You want to get yourself into a position where you can afford to buy those properties. And then focus on the growth you can get from them and how that will help you achieve your wealth-creation goals.

Case study

Starting again to set up three kids

Daniel came to me when he was 49. He had previously owned an interstate light transport business but during the COVID-19 pandemic, he lost a lot of business and the business never really recovered.

Once he had liquidated the business and paid off some debt, he had $630 000 left, as well as some money in a self-managed super fund. Once he got a job as a PAYG employee, he had a borrowing capacity of $850 000 and a total budget of $1 480 000. While that might appear healthy, Daniel needed to spread this over more than one property purchase if he was to reach his goal of setting up for life his three Brisbane-based kids, aged 12, 15 and 18.

The strategy was to buy properties Daniel could afford and that the kids could eventually move into. One is moving to Sydney

(continued)

to study in two years' time, so that determined where we needed to buy the first property.

Property 1: Rockdale, Sydney

With our help, Daniel bought a two-bedroom unit with secure lock-up parking in Rockdale:

- *Purchase price:* $650 000
- *Bedrooms: 2; bathrooms:* 2; secure parking
- *Location:* Rockdale, Sydney
- *Rental income:* $750 a week
- *Yield:* 6 per cent (very good for Sydney)
- *Purpose:* to house his daughter who is moving to Sydney to study.

Properties 2 and 3: New Farm, Brisbane

We bought two further units in Brisbane because they suited Daniel's budget. Brisbane was already booming, and houses would have been too expensive. We chose New Farm, close to the CBD.

Each unit cost under $600 000 and the cash flow on them is really strong because there's a massive shortage of supply:

- *Purchase price:* under $600 000 each
- *Bedrooms:* 1
- *Location:* New Farm, Brisbane (a solid inner-city area)
- *Rental income:* Just under $600 a week each

Strong cash flow due to a shortage of available housing in the area and high rental demand.

Daniel's cash-flow strategy

Because Daniel's kids are young, he's going to rent these properties out for now so he'll have cash flow as well as some capital growth.

The ultimate goal is that when his kids move out of home, or when they need to get established, they'll each have an apartment waiting.

In the meantime, strong cash flow will help pay down the debt. By the time the kids need these properties, the mortgages will be significantly reduced if not paid off entirely.

How Daniel's property-investing budget was allocated

Total budget: $1 480 000 ($630 000 cash + $850 000 borrowing capacity)

- *Property 1 (Sydney):* $650 000
- *Property 2 (Brisbane):* ~$600 000
- *Property 3 (Brisbane):* ~$600 000
- *Total spent:* approximately $1 850 000
- *Remaining capacity:* reserved for SMSF property purchase (but with a separate deposit and borrowing capacity for the SMSF).

Setting himself up: SMSF property

While Daniel's setting his kids up, he's planning an SMSF property purchase in the first quarter of 2027 to ensure he has something for his retirement through his self-managed super fund.

(continued)

Daniel's timeline

Here's how the strategy we devised with Daniel will play out over time:

- Right now: All three properties are rented and generating strong cash flow.
- In two years: Daniel's eldest son (now 18) will move to Sydney for study and live in the Rockdale apartment.
- In five or six years: Daniel's middle son (now 15) potentially lives in one of the Brisbane apartments.
- In 10 years: The other Brisbane apartment will be available for Daniel's youngest son (now 12).
- Throughout: Cash flow pays down all three mortgages, and the properties continue to grow in value.
- By the time each child needs their property, significant equity will have been built.

The outcome

Daniel has turned his situation around completely. Instead of dwelling on what he lost, he used what he had left to secure his own and his children's futures.

Daniel's three kids won't have to struggle to get into the market as so many young people do. And in the meantime, all three properties are generating cash flow that's helping pay down the debt. And he's setting himself up for retirement.

That's what I call turning a difficult situation into a strategic opportunity.

Lloyd's top tips for property investors

I have given you a lot of information in this chapter, but in a nutshell these are the things I tell my clients, and what I do myself.

1. **Do your research.** Don't buy the first property you see. Look at the history of the suburb, check out the growth for both houses and units, find out what's driving the market. Use tools such as RP Data or PriceFinder, and if you're working with a broker or buyer's agent, get them to spit out the numbers for you.
2. **Do your due diligence.** If you're thinking of buying a unit, always get a strata report before making an offer. Check whether there have been any special levies in the past; whether there are upcoming big expenses; and whether there's sufficient money in the strata's sinking fund or body corporate. You don't want any nasty surprises down the track.
3. **Know the likely net yield.** Gross yields look good on paper, but it's the *net* yield that matters. Factor in all your fees — strata, council and water rates, insurances and any special levies. The numbers may not be as strong as they first appear, so always crunch them properly.
4. **Understand the purpose of each property in terms of your overall plan.** Every property in your portfolio should have a purpose. Is it for growth or yield, or is it a stepping stone to something bigger? Don't buy for the sake of buying — make sure it fits your overall strategy.
5. **Don't overthink.** The market moves quickly, and the best opportunities go to those who are prepared and decisive. Do your research then don't be afraid to buy when the time

(continued)

is right. Don't get stuck waiting for the perfect property at the perfect time and let great opportunities pass you by.

6. **Work with professionals.** Use experts who understand the market and can guide you confidently and objectively. A good broker, buyer's agent and accountant can save you headaches and help you make smarter investment decisions.
7. **Review your portfolio regularly.** Markets change, and so will your goals. Keep an eye on your properties. Check they're still performing well and don't be afraid to adjust your strategy.

Where are you now?

Let's break this down by what stage of life or investment you're at. The next chapter is for twenty-somethings and those with low income but a good freedom fund. Then I'll speak to thirty-somethings who are tempted to buy their dream home, time-poor forty- to fifty-somethings and, last but not least, empty nesters and retirees.

Key takeaways

- Median property prices in Australia are high by world standards but not necessarily out of reach for those who think strategically.
- Despite high entry prices, Australia ticks a lot of the boxes for international investors.
- Your best chance of success is not by outspending competitors but by outstrategising them.
- Do your research and due diligence, follow your plan and don't overthink.
- Diversify your portfolio, spreading your risk across cities and regions, price brackets and property types.
- Look beyond big cities to emerging outer suburbs and regional towns that can deliver equally good growth and yield.

Chapter 7

Get on the ladder to financial freedom

This chapter is aimed primarily at first-property buyers — twenty-somethings, and even precocious aspiring investors still at school. I'll run through some clear steps to take to set yourself up for life, even if you're on an entry-level wage or early in your career. If early retirement sounds good to you, jump in.

A lot of really young people — 16, 17 and 18 years old — come to me expressing an interest in property having read my books, and I've made it a mission to inform them about finance, property and investment. I've always been interested in this — it's one of the reasons I wrote this book.

Having been a school music teacher, I know schools don't prepare kids with a proper financial education. Their emphasis is on getting good marks in your school certificate or HSC — whatever the system where you live — then going on to uni and getting a degree. The target is to get a good job, buy a home and work your whole life.

You're not taught about how to manage your finances or how you won't become wealthy simply by saving what you earn after buying one home. You have to learn how to invest—essentially, to create more wealth.

Whether you bought it yourself, you're studying it at school or your parents introduced you to it, this book is for you as much as for them. I've got to say, though, Gen Z is really onto it these days. Books, podcasts and social media are all contributing to this shift. And I want to thank you for getting off the socials and reading a book on property investment and how to set yourself up for life.

There's definitely more information on property out there now, and more talk around the possibility of retiring early. Young people often come to me either because they want to work for me as a stepping stone to becoming a property mogul, or looking to set themselves up for life with 20 properties.

I mentioned that I was 28 before I bought my first property. When I was a teacher I couldn't see how I was going to set myself up at all, though I always had that dream home in my mind. I was fortunate to be teaching at some nice schools around Sydney's eastern suburbs. People had these massive houses with swimming pools and nice cars. It opened my eyes. I thought, how do these people afford this life?

If I were starting my property journey again today, I'd definitely do some things differently. The first thing I'd do is seek authoritative advice, just as you are doing right now, and just as I didn't do my first time around.

And this is the kind of advice I could have used.

Don't live in your property

I lived in my first property for about five years. It was a new apartment—not bought off-the-plan but newly built—well located only by chance because I bought in the suburb I already lived in, Rockdale. I didn't think I could have bought further afield—let alone in another state or region—because at the time I had no real interest in or knowledge about property; I was just teaching. But after about five years as a homeowner I caught the investment bug. I thought, what if I tried to buy another property?

I thought I'd sell my Rockdale apartment and buy something bigger. But then I spoke to my mortgage broker and read a few articles and realised that I didn't have to sell my first property in order to buy a second one.

So I got finance for another property, bought it, moved into it, then used Rockdale as an investment and rented it out. I lived in that second property for a couple of years before I moved into *another* property I'd bought and rented out my second property.

The problem with that approach was that I kept buying properties to live in, *before* they became investments. That's not a very good strategy. Also, they were all in Sydney, not in suburbs that made much sense from an investment perspective. They were simply decent properties in areas I was familiar with and could afford at the time.

As I've noted, a far better option is to rentvest.

Back when I bought that first apartment, I could have *rented* in Rockdale or somewhere close by, then *bought* real-estate investments that made sense—around the country rather than just in Sydney.

That way I could have benefited from the strong growth markets and enjoyed the same lifestyle in inner Sydney.

Eventually I discovered the power of building duplexes, which helped accelerate my journey. It also got me out of the habit of only buying homes to live in.

That's also when I started to invest in different markets. I bought my first Brisbane property and did some investing in the Newcastle market. I expanded into new areas and built my portfolio from there.

Not long after that I decided that teaching forever wasn't for me. I really wanted a plan that enabled me to retire from teaching early and do the property thing full-time. From the time I bought my first property to when I stopped teaching probably 13 years had passed. But I think if I'd had smart strategies in place from the start, I would have achieved the same result in just nine or 10 years.

The key takeaway here is that once I had the right strategies in place, I managed to reach my passive income goal, which was basically to replace my teaching income, quite quickly. Then I was able to retire from teaching and just keep investing in property.

Ninety per cent of investors never get that second property

Goals are a big thing. You need to keep your 'perfect day' top of mind to remind you of *why* you're saving for that first deposit. It's to get you onto the property ladder, your first step to financial freedom and your dream lifestyle. You need to envisage what that long-term future looks like, and what you're going to do with that property in five years' time.

When I invest, I always look at the property I plan to purchase and, first, consider how it's going to help me get into my next property. Because you don't want to be part of the 90 per cent of Australian investors who *never get past one property*. So you need to make sure you invest in property that will help you move forward.

Someone who spends their entire budget on one property is likely to end up in that 90 per cent. You might have a million-dollar budget, but if you spend it all on one property, and that property has a really low yield—say, it brings in $600 a week in rent—you're completely maxed out, with no serviceability left for your next purchase.

The percentage of investors owning multiple properties drops with every additional property. Very few investors own two, let alone three, four or 10 properties.

Why do most investors stop at one?

Well, a common reason is that prospective property investors either buy the wrong property first up or have the wrong financial structure in place.

The wrong property for your strategy might be one that maxes out your budget and gets you stuck. It could be a house-and-land package or an off-the-plan apartment that's tied up all your funds. It might be something like my property in Blackwater—an investment that hasn't performed well and leaves you without the equity you need to move forward.

Why time is your best ally

Time is the one thing you can never get back. Buy at the age of 20, and you'll have 30-plus years for compounding growth and loan paydowns to work in your favour.

For a young person who wants to retire early, it comes down to their income and what they want out of retirement. A young person who wants to retire by age 30 isn't going to be in the same position as someone who's been working their whole life, has more money and can retire at 60.

Again, it comes down to goals and what you're trying to achieve. Then we reverse-engineer that. So the first question I ask my clients is where they want to be in five, 10, 15 years' time. Then I try to understand what they're trying to achieve, and look at the budget and income they have.

Often people say, 'I want to buy my own home.' And I say, 'Yeah, but it's probably not a good idea to buy that now.'

If someone says they want to buy a property to live in, I'll always ask them whether that actually aligns with what they're trying to achieve over the long term. Buying your own place isn't necessarily a bad move, but it can eat into your borrowing capacity, which can limit your ability to move forward with further investments.

Typically, banks will lend you more once you've got an investment property with rent coming in, because they know you'll have to pay less out of your own pocket to service that loan.

So if you diligently pay off the mortgage on your principal place of residence (PPOR) straight away, all that happens is that you get stuck, unable to borrow. That's the whole reason people end up with their paid-off family home and nothing else.

There are also no tax deductions on a property that's also your own home, so financially it doesn't work the same way as an investment property, and people can sometimes find themselves financially stuck as a result.

So if someone comes to me saying they want to generate, say, $100 000 a year in passive income from property, but they want to buy their own home first, I try to show them that those two goals don't always line up. If you've got an investment property, and it's neutral or positively geared, then you're not actually paying for it; the rent's paying for it.

If passive income is the priority, then you generally need to focus on investing first. The dream home comes later.

An emotional purchase

Maybe you are under pressure to buy property to live in instead of renting. But let's remember that your ultimate goal isn't just to own a home. It's to set yourself up for life. Buying a home won't necessarily achieve that.

Often people just do that because they're following a traditional life path: go to university, get a job, take out a mortgage, buy a house and spend the next 30 years paying it off. At the end of it you own a house, but you may have spent your entire working life just servicing that debt. That's a model we're trying to move beyond.

The other thing to remember is that *a principal place of residence is usually an emotional purchase.* If someone comes in with, say, $1.5 million in borrowing capacity, there's a strong impulse for them to use all of it if they're buying their own home—especially if it's in a capital city, where that's often what it takes just to get into the market. But once they've done that they have no free money to invest elsewhere.

With that same borrowing capacity, you could potentially buy two or three investment properties around the country. That way, you'd be generating cash flow right from the start, getting onto the property ladder, benefiting from capital growth and actively building wealth.

Tempting as it may be to make your first property purchase your home, it's not usually the smartest way to financial freedom.

Most people starting out can't afford to buy their ideal home in a location they love, anyway. So I say, 'Rent a nice place in a suburb you like. As time passes that investment property will start paying itself off, your equity in it will grow, and you can use some of that equity to borrow more and invest in a second investment property as you continue to rent. All the time you're getting closer to your goal of financial freedom.'

When the time's right, you'll be able to afford that dream home—and you won't get stuck in the meantime. With a strategy like this, you'll potentially be able to buy a much better home later on, rather than stretching yourself to buy something today that isn't all you'd want it to be anyhow. Because right now you simply can't afford your dream home.

How to buy your PPOR

When Renee and I bought our dream home in Lilli Pilli I sold a couple of properties to help buy it. I sold a property in Newcastle and another in Sydney's inner west and used the profits to help pay for our dream home.

I was able to put down a 50 per cent deposit because of the position I'm in with my portfolio. When I was younger I was putting down a 5 per cent or 10 per cent deposit.

Today a 10 per cent deposit on a decent city home would require the average young person to clean out all their savings. If instead, they bought an affordable investment property initially, they could then use the equity from that property to help them buy their own, much better home in five or 10 years' time, even in today's property markets. And because you're buying in more affordable property markets initially, you can put a higher deposit down, which keeps your mortgage smaller, so you're paying less interest too.

Hence you get more equity in your place more quickly, which puts you in a much more comfortable situation faster and means you'll be able to buy a bigger home sooner.

Case study

Using time to their advantage

Matt and Lauren, in their late twenties, came to us with a borrowing capacity of only $600 000. That's not a huge amount to work with, especially if you're trying to build a property portfolio.

(continued)

The good thing for this couple was that they were prepared to start early and use the one big advantage they had — time.

Their other advantage was that they had clear goals:

- Retire early so they can spend time on their hobbies.
- Use investments to build up passive income and a freedom fund.
- Ultimate goal: finance their dream home through investments.

Given their limited borrowing capacity, to help Matt and Lauren move forward we had to focus on cash flow. If you can't borrow much, you need your properties to pay for themselves, and ideally contribute positively to your cash flow so you can build capacity for the next purchase.

The property

- *Purchase price:* $495 000
- *Location:* regional Queensland
- *Type:* residential
- *Initial gross yield:* 6 per cent
- *Post-renovation yield:* 7 per cent
- *Strategy:* strong cash flow + cosmetic renovation

We found them a property in regional Queensland that was going to give them that 6 per cent yield straight away. But we didn't stop there. After six months they completed a $22 000 cosmetic renovation (figures 7.1 and 7.2).

That renovation bumped the yield up to 7 per cent, and the property became positively geared after the renovation. That meant it was putting money in their pocket every week, not taking it out.

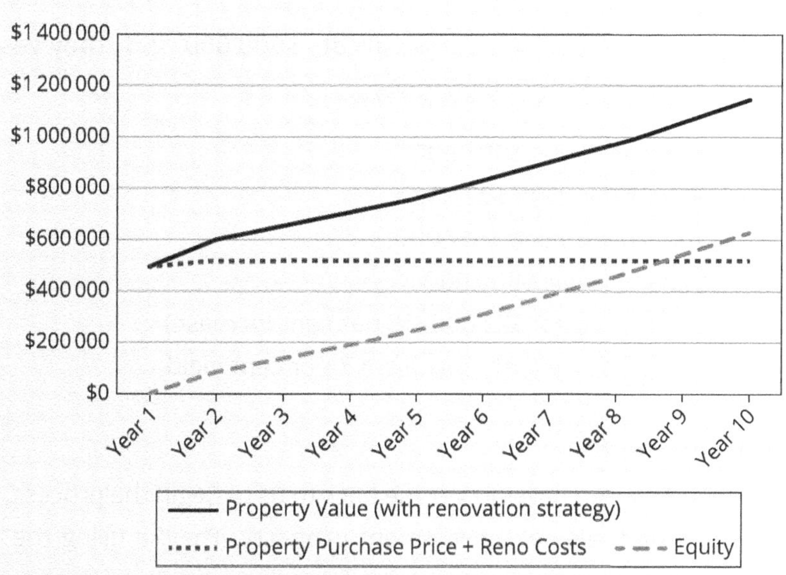

Figure 7.1 ***Matt and Lauren's renovation strategy over time***

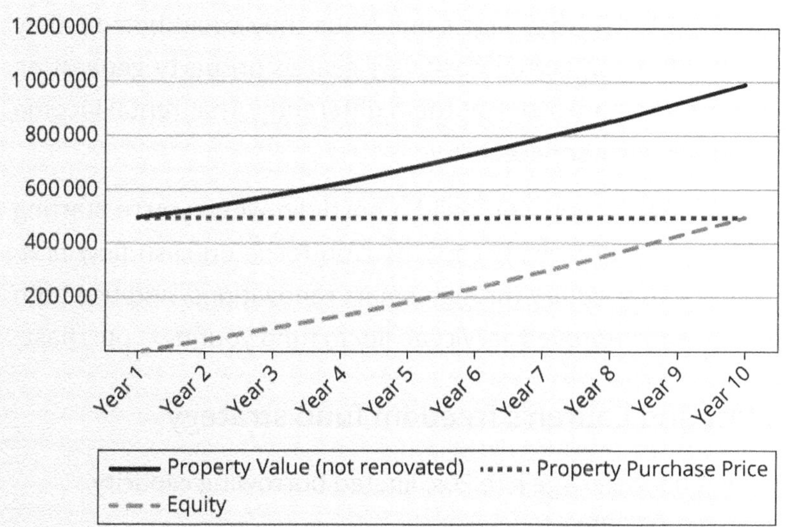

Figure 7.2 ***What they could have expected without renovation***

(continued)

The results

The latest valuation came in at $600 000. So they've manufactured $105 000 in equity.

- *Purchase price:* $495 000
- *Renovation cost:* $22 000
- *Total investment:* $517 000
- *Current value:* $600 000
- *Equity created:* $83 000 (16 per cent increase)
- *Plus:* positive cash flow from 7 per cent yield

What's next

Matt and Lauren have now come back to us to begin the process of securing their next investment property. They're using the equity from their first purchase to fund the deposit.

The increased cash flow has also helped their borrowing capacity. When they first came to us they could borrow only $600 000. Now, with a positively geared property generating income, the banks look at them differently. That rental income improves their serviceability.

This is exactly how you build a portfolio when you're starting with limited borrowing capacity. You focus on cash flow first, manufacture equity through smart renovations, and use both equity and improved serviceability to fund your next purchase.

Matt and Lauren's freedom fund strategy

- *Challenge:* Age late 20s, limited borrowing capacity ($600 000)
- *Goal:* Build passive income and eventually fund their dream home

- *Strategy:* High-yield regional property plus cosmetic renovation to boost cash flow and equity
- *Focus:* Positive gearing first to improve serviceability and borrowing power
- *Result:* $83 000 equity created and stronger borrowing position for the next purchase
- *Next phase:* Use equity and improved cash flow to secure the second investment property
- *Key takeaway:* When borrowing capacity is tight, prioritising cash flow and manufactured equity can fast-track portfolio growth.

Fast-track your deposit

One of the biggest advantages you have as a young person is that you typically have lower living costs than someone in their forties. If you're single or a couple, you can do a lot of things to save money and build up that deposit quickly.

The great thing with property is that you only need to save for the first deposit. Once your first property grows in value you'll be able to access that equity and use it to purchase subsequent properties. That's how you grow a portfolio.

It all stems from being able to save enough for the deposit on your first property purchase. So what can you do, starting today, to help build that initial deposit?

Side hustles and additional income

A few 25-year-olds might be lucky enough to earn $300 000 a year, but most aren't. So from a property investing perspective one of the biggest things you can do early on is increase your income.

That doesn't mean everyone needs to quit their job and launch a business; sometimes it's simply about creating extra income on the side. An additional income source can directly increase your borrowing capacity and give you more options for investing.

Even a small side hustle can make a meaningful difference to your investment capacity. Extra income means you may be able to borrow more from the bank. If you're earning $60 000 and you add a side hustle that brings in $40 000, suddenly you're into six figures. You can do a lot more with that level of income than you can with $60 000 alone. You can take it to a mortgage broker, and potentially increase your borrowing capacity. That, in turn, opens the door to further property investment.

In my experience, young people are more likely to be open to the side-hustle strategy—and to have the energy for it. You might still be living with your parents and working two jobs. Plenty of people do that.

Rather than getting a second job—which is essentially just trading hours for money—some people work on building a business with the potential to become a second income stream. Ideally it's also something you're genuinely interested in, because I don't think anyone should run a business they're not passionate about.

While it has its risks, this path, if it pays off, can help you fast-track your way to a deposit. I'll tell you more about how I did this in chapter 11.

There are lots of potential strategies for boosting your income, so you can fast-track saving for that initial deposit. However you decide to do it, the underlying idea is that *growing your income expands your investment options.*

Income growth over time

You won't be in your twenties or early thirties forever. Right now, you're probably not earning much compared to what you will be, 10 or 20 years down the track. You might still be studying full time and working part time. If, say, you're a recent uni graduate or have just qualified in a trade: you might be earning only $50 000 or $60 000 a year, but it's likely you'll earn more once you gain some experience and get a promotion or two. So if a 20-year-old tells me they want to retire in 20 years' time, I can't use their current income as the benchmark. Their income is almost certain to increase over time.

As people reach their late twenties or early thirties, it's quite common for their income to have doubled from their entry-level earnings. So growth in income also needs to be factored into long-term property planning.

Couples: the same strategy applies

In this conversation I'm not just talking to single people; I'm also referring to young couples looking to invest.

These days even a double income may not add up to much. A young couple might both be working, but their combined annual income might still be less than $150 000. Even if a couple came to me with a combined income of $400 000, I'd probably recommend the same thing, which is that they rentvest and get a couple of investment properties before buying their own home.

Because typically what people with that level of salary *want* to do is to buy a bigger house in an affluent city suburb.

This book isn't about living large to outshine the next guy before you can really afford it, and then getting stuck in a high-spending rut. It's about becoming *set for life*. You're not setting yourself up for life if you're under 40 and already trying to buy your dream home before you're even on the first rung of the investment property ladder.

The bottom line is, whether you're a single person, with or without a side hustle, or a dual-income couple, I recommend you *invest* your money.

Accept the trade-offs

This is the point at which most prospective property investors fail. The reality is that to achieve financial freedom, *you will need to sacrifice some short-term fun*. That might mean renting for a few more years, having fewer nights out, fewer holidays, secondhand cars and so on—but to my mind, that's a small price to pay for decades of financial freedom.

The advantage of having investment properties is that *they pay themselves off*. And once they're paid off they pay you an income. Yes, there's some upkeep, but everything's tax-deductible: all the interest, council rates, maintenance, repairs. By contrast, nothing associated with the upkeep of your own home is tax-deductible.

The fact is that from a financial perspective the system tends to favour property investors over homeowners.

Both sides of first home buyer schemes

One of the biggest advantages for young people is access to first-home buyer incentives. These incentives mean you pay no stamp duty when buying a property (if the property meets certain criteria), which can save you a considerable amount of money.

In late 2025 the federal government rolled out an expanded 5 per cent deposit scheme for first-home buyers. Under the earlier scheme, people buying property needed to put down a 20 per cent deposit for it. Now buyers can put down a 5 per cent deposit and the government will guarantee the other 15 per cent. For single parents the deposit can be as low as 2 per cent!

There are clear advantages to this:

- A 5 per cent deposit instead of 20 per cent will reduce the deposit-savings timeline.
- No lenders mortgage insurance can save buyers $20 000 to $60 000 in extra costs.
- With no income caps or limits, the scheme is open to a wider group of buyers.
- Higher property price caps: in Sydney it applies to properties priced at up to $1.5 million; in Melbourne it's $950 000; in both Brisbane and Canberra it's $1 million. In other capitals, the price caps are a bit lower, with Adelaide at $900 000, Perth at $850 000 and Hobart at $700 000.

But there are also some big concerns that could offset those positives:

- **Rising prices.** With more buyers able to purchase, competition increases. Analysts are already warning that property values could rise as a result.
- **Bigger mortgages.** A smaller deposit means borrowing more, which can make repayments tougher if interest rates change.
- **Rushed decisions.** When opportunities like this open up, buyers often panic, compromise on quality and/or pay more than a property is worth.
- **Additional costs.** Even if buyers only have to put 5 per cent of the property's purchase price down, stamp duty, legal fees and moving expenses may still apply.

I've been to auctions recently with price guides of $1.2 to $1.3 million, which is reasonably cheap for Sydney. However, in some cases, those properties actually sold for $400 000 to $500 000 above the price guide. Everything has been pushed up in value, and there's strong demand.

To my mind, the bigger issue is the housing shortage. Under the National Housing Accord, the federal government was set to build 1.2 million houses over the five years to 2030, but as yet we're nowhere near that total. So what we're really seeing is a shortage of houses, insufficient infrastructure in the outer suburbs of cities and too much 'red tape' around council approvals.

And in my opinion, this 5 per cent scheme—while it has some positives—is contributing to the problem.

Drawbacks of the 5 per cent deposit

I don't actively advise people to use the 5 per cent deposit scheme. People come to me already thinking about it. They've heard it's a way to get into the market sooner, with less savings upfront, and on the surface that sounds attractive.

Even though, nowadays, around 90 per cent of our clients are investors, lately some of them have been asking about the 5 per cent scheme. They feel it's cheaper to get into property with a smaller deposit. And because the scheme allows them to buy sooner, they assume it must be the better option.

The catch is that to use the scheme you typically need to live in the property.

Take Sydney, as an example: if someone wants to buy there with a budget of under a million dollars, using a 5 per cent deposit, they don't have a huge range of choices. Often they'll end up looking at smaller apartments, sometimes one-bedroom units, simply because that's what fits both their budget and the scheme's requirements.

You need to ask yourself, 'What property is actually going to serve me best over the long term?' Because the same savings that allow a 5 per cent deposit in Sydney could potentially fund a 10 per cent deposit somewhere else, on an investment-grade property. That might well be a bigger, better property in a regional market—say, in an area just over an hour's drive from Melbourne and close to the coast, like Geelong; or in go-ahead parts of Queensland; or in the outer suburbs of Brisbane—places where houses, not just apartments, may still be accessible to first-home buyers.

Those properties might not suit those buying them as places to live, but there's a good chance they'll have stronger long-term growth prospects. And that's really what I focus on. I always look at the data first, then weigh up whether the short-term saving from a 5 per cent deposit actually stacks up against the long-term potential of the asset.

On the flip side, you might buy a property simply because you can, under the 5 per cent deposit scheme, have to live in it (so no rental income), and then find—particularly if it's a smaller apartment with weaker historical growth or potential strata issues—that the capital growth is limited. And once you've bought, you're committed to that asset for a significant period of time, because buying and selling have associated costs so you can't do it too often.

Saving a few thousand dollars upfront can feel significant at the time, but those initial savings can pale into insignificance if the alternative property generates substantially more equity over the next decade.

A standalone house: what is the minimum?

I always recommend that people buy standalone houses, if possible, as a quality investment, but by the start of 2026 you could no longer do that in Sydney's metro area for under $1 million. In Sydney, almost anywhere, you'd be struggling to get a two-bedroom apartment for under a million.

By late 2025 Brisbane's median house price had reached over $1.1 million, with some reports placing it closer to $1.13 million, overtaking Melbourne and Canberra. But you can still find a standalone house for under a million in the outer suburbs of Newcastle and in many suburbs on NSW's Central Coast, 1.5 to 2.5 hours' drive north of Sydney. In Geelong, only 70 kilometres from Melbourne, you could still locate standalone houses for $650 000 to $700 000.

So don't think you have to have a million dollars in borrowing capacity to buy a good standalone house that will bring in a decent rental return and appreciate well over time. You'll just have to look outside most of the major capital cities to find it.

Think small but smart

Your first property doesn't need to be flash. A modest regional house is fine if it gets you into the market. What's important is that you actually take that first step.

No-one has ever built wealth by sitting on the sidelines waiting for the perfect moment. You don't become rich by doing nothing. Generally, you're better off entering the market as soon as you can afford to rather than trying to second-guess what it might do next.

People often think, I'll wait 12 months and interest rates might come down and my borrowing capacity will improve. And sure, that might happen. But if rates fall, markets can move quickly too. Increased borrowing capacity often brings increased competition, and prices can rise just as fast. No-one has a crystal ball so trying to time the market perfectly is incredibly difficult, even for seasoned investors.

So tick off all the steps I've given you so far and trust your instincts. Read on to see where your property adventure might take you.

Key takeaways

- Think small, but smart. Your first property doesn't need to be flash. What's important is to take that first step. No-one has ever built wealth by sitting on the sidelines waiting for the perfect moment.
- Don't live in your property — rentvesting is a better strategy by far.
- After the first one, invest in different markets to reduce the risk and help you move forward.
- Time, and the power of compound interest, are your best allies.
- Once you've saved for that first deposit you're on your way.

Chapter 8

Build a portfolio that advances your goals

People in their thirties sometimes panic because they feel they aren't ticking enough boxes. Maybe their friends are getting married and buying their first home. I felt like that in my early thirties. By the time I met Renee I was 36 and already set up financially, so things worked out.

In hindsight, I think the most important thing is to find the right life partner, and you don't want to rush that decision! Just believe it'll happen when it does and in the meantime keep working towards your goals.

I know that when you're in your thirties, the pressure from friends and family to buy that first home can increase, but my advice in chapter 7 holds true. Don't rush into the first property you can afford just because your friends are real-estate obsessed.

Owning—and having a mortgage on—the property you call home is usually not the smartest move financially. That's particularly true if you have cost-of-living pressures and limited income. Unless you're a builder who is happy to upgrade the property you're living in before flipping it for a good profit, *you're much better off rentvesting.*

You can still focus on rentvesting if you're married with kids. These days, it's common to continue renting well into your thirties and beyond, partly so you can live where you choose to, whether that's close to the beach or close to work.

If you have already purchased a property, now may be the time to think about your next move. In chapter 7 we talked about how to avoid getting stuck with a huge owner-occupier mortgage that will stop you from doing that.

Use equity to grow your portfolio

Once you've bought your first property, the next question is usually, 'How do I keep moving forward without saving another full deposit from scratch?' This is where understanding the power of equity to build your portfolio comes into play.

As we discussed in earlier chapters, equity is the difference between what your property is worth and what you owe on it. If you bought a property for $600 000 and it's now worth $750 000, you've potentially built $150 000 in equity. That doesn't mean you have $150 000 sitting in the bank, but it does mean you may be able to access some of it to fund your next purchase.

Equity can grow as property values rise over time, or it can be manufactured. In the latter case, you actively increase value through renovations, further development or by strategically buying below market value.

To access equity, you will usually refinance with your lender or with another bank. The bank will reassess your property's value and your lending position, and if there's sufficient equity and serviceability, you may be able to release funds to use as a deposit on another property. Most lenders will allow borrowing up to around 80 per cent of the property's value without requiring lenders mortgage insurance, so that usually determines how much usable equity is available.

But here's the important part. You access equity not to spend it but to redeploy it into income-producing assets. Using equity to upgrade cars, take holidays or fund lifestyle expenses doesn't build long-term wealth. Using equity to acquire assets that generate cash flow and growth, on the other hand, accelerates your freedom fund.

A well-structured portfolio often grows in stages:

- The first property builds initial equity.
- That equity helps fund the next purchase.
- Additional properties create more income and borrowing capacity.
- Over time, assets are consolidated, debt is reduced or properties are sold strategically to strengthen cash flow.

Many investors use this strategy to create a portfolio of several properties without needing enormous savings upfront.

Of course, equity alone isn't enough. You still need serviceability, which is the capacity to comfortably repay loans. That's why balancing growth properties with cash-flow ones can be so powerful. Strong rental income helps support future borrowing and reduces financial stress.

And remember, accessing equity should always align with your broader strategy. It's not about accumulating properties for the sake of it. It's about building a portfolio that supports your long-term goals, which might include generating passive income, financial flexibility or eventually funding your dream home without excessive debt.

Used wisely, equity becomes a tool that keeps your portfolio moving forward. Used poorly, it can slow you down.

The key is having a clear plan.

Negative vs positive gearing

The tax strategy around your investment property really depends on your goals, because, broadly speaking, you can buy either negatively geared or positively geared property. One approach isn't necessarily better than the other. It comes down to what you're trying to achieve, where you're at financially and how good your cash flow is.

Negative gearing refers to investment in a property whose income doesn't cover its expenses. That shortfall, usually made up of interest payments, maintenance costs, insurance and management fees, can usually be used to reduce your taxable income, which is why higher-income earners often make negatively geared property part of their strategy.

The trade-off is that you'll tip money into the property each month in the expectation that eventually long-term capital growth will more than compensate for short-term losses. Many blue-chip metropolitan properties fall into this category because they're bought primarily for long-term growth rather than instant income.

Positive gearing is the opposite. The rental income covers all the expenses and produces surplus cash flow. This extra income can help with living expenses, accelerate debt repayment or fund additional investments. For people starting out, those with limited borrowing capacity or those approaching retirement, positively geared property can provide much-needed financial breathing room. A property can have slightly negative cash flow but after a tax refund can work out as positive.

Of course, the tax implications differ. You'll pay tax on the income generated by a positively geared property. But in practical terms, most investors would rather pay tax on profits than claim deductions on losses. Cash flow gives you financial flexibility while tax deductions merely soften the impact of expenses. But whether an investment property is negatively or positively geared, most expenses associated with it are tax-deductible. These typically include mortgage interest, council and water rates, strata fees, property management costs, insurance, maintenance and repairs.

Many investors use both strategies successfully, particularly as growth-focused negatively geared properties may become neutral or positive over time as rents increase and loans are paid down. Meanwhile, higher-yield properties can support cash flow and improve borrowing capacity for further acquisitions.

Think of gearing as part of a broader portfolio strategy. Early in your investing journey, you might prioritise growth. Later, as retirement approaches, cash flow can become more important. We'll cover those scenarios in later chapters.

Positive cash flow plays a decisive role in growing your portfolio because it improves your borrowing capacity and reduces financial pressure. If a property puts money in your pocket rather than taking it out, banks will see you as a lower risk when you want to secure finance for the next purchase. And because you're not constantly dipping into your salary or savings to hold the property, you can keep building momentum. Over time, strong cash flow can fund deposits, cover expenses and give you the confidence to keep expanding your portfolio strategically.

Ultimately, the goal isn't just tax efficiency. It's building a portfolio that supports your freedom fund by balancing growth, income, risk and lifestyle goals over the long term.

Location

As covered in chapter 6, property markets in Australia are influenced by local factors that include economic conditions, population growth and government policies. Investing in a range of types of property across a range of locations spreads your risk by reducing your exposure to localised market downturns.

Should one property underperform or another be vacant for a time, others in your portfolio can cushion you from losses. Such a strategy not only safeguards your assets overall but positions you to capitalise on multiple growth opportunities across the broad real-estate market.

Investing across states and territories also allows you to take advantage of property cycles, another strategy discussed in chapter 6. That means you can purchase in markets poised for growth at the same time as others may be peaking or declining. It's a strategy that can lead to more consistent capital growth over time.

It's important to be aware that each state or territory in Australia has its own rules and regulations for buying property and for tax on property investments. By owning properties in multiple states, you can potentially stay below the land-tax threshold in each, minimising your overall tax liability. The savings can be significant, especially as your portfolio grows.

Property types

Choosing property types is an important part of building a portfolio, but it's something investors often overlook. Houses, townhouses and apartments each behave differently in terms of growth, rental income and long-term performance. While no single option is perfect, understanding the strengths and trade-offs of each can help you make smarter decisions.

I tend to favour houses because of the land component. Land is one of the key drivers of long-term capital growth. It appreciates over time while buildings depreciate and while you can renovate or rebuild a house, you can't create more land. Apartment buildings, on the other hand, can continue to be built upwards, which can limit price growth if supply keeps increasing.

That doesn't mean units are necessarily a bad investment. In fact, sometimes they're the most practical entry point. Take Sydney. You might see houses with rental yields of only 2 or 3 per cent in some premium suburbs, meaning they are likely to be heavily negatively geared. Meanwhile, a well-located apartment in the same area might deliver a 4 to 4.5 per cent yield. While an apartment may not have the long-term land appreciation a house has, it can still provide solid growth while being much easier to hold financially. And of course the entry price is much lower.

Townhouses often sit somewhere between apartments and standalone houses. They usually include some land and may offer better yields and have lower maintenance demands than houses. Many investors choose types of property that allow them to strike a balance between growth potential, affordability and maintenance.

Buying the ideal property isn't always realistic, as servicing the loan is critical and mortgage repayments that drain your cash flow can prevent you from acquiring further assets and stall your overall progress. Building a portfolio isn't, then, just about buying the best properties on paper; it's about buying assets you can hold sustainably.

This is one reason I recommend regional cities. As I've noted, you can often secure a full house on a good block of land and achieve rental yields of around 5 per cent or more. A combination of land value and cash flow can help support portfolio growth without excessive financial strain.

Your personal financial position plays a big role in the type of property you choose. High-income earners might comfortably hold a negatively geared house in a capital city because their income supports it and the tax deductions help soften the impact. But most investors need stronger cash flow, especially early on, if they are to maintain borrowing capacity and keep expanding their portfolio.

So there isn't a right or wrong property type. The key is to align a property with your income, your borrowing capacity and your long-term goals.

Why buy investment-grade properties?

An investment-grade property is one that is likely to outperform the average property in its suburb over the long term. It doesn't just benefit from general market growth; it tends to attract stronger demand, more reliable tenants and better resale interest. It's the kind of property people genuinely want to live in, not just the one investors settle for because it's affordable.

When you look at any suburb, you'll notice properties on noisy main roads or near commercial activity or in less appealing positions often lag behind even when the overall market is strong. On the other hand, properties in particular streets, near good schools, hospitals, transport links and lifestyle amenities, often hold their value better and grow faster than properties in less desirable pockets. Buyers may see renovation potential or development options. A practical floorplan also makes a difference, as homes that are functional and adaptable tend to attract a wider buyer pool.

Another factor I always consider is how a property will perform when the market slows down. In a booming market, almost any property will sell. There's momentum, competition and plenty of buyers. But when conditions tighten, the gap between average properties and investment-grade properties becomes very clear. Properties lacking strong fundamentals can sit on the market longer, leading to price reductions, or struggle to attract serious buyers.

This is where thinking about the *future buyer* is critical. When you eventually sell, whether that's in five, 10 or 20 years, you want your property to appeal to both owner-occupiers and investors. The broader the appeal, the stronger your resale position.

One useful metric when researching suburbs is the owner-occupier-to-renter ratio. Ideally, you're looking for areas with roughly 70 to 80 per cent owner-occupiers and 20 to 30 per cent renters. High owner-occupier areas often display better maintenance, stronger community stability and better long-term capital growth prospects.

You can find this data through property research platforms, government census data and free sites like realestate.com.au. A good buyer's agent will also analyse these statistics for you as part of their due diligence.

Ultimately, buying investment-grade property isn't about buying the most expensive house. It's about buying the best-quality asset you can comfortably hold. That balance is crucial. A premium asset that strains your finances too much can slow your portfolio growth, while a cheaper but well-chosen property can still perform strongly over time.

The goal, as always, is to build a portfolio that supports your freedom fund—assets that grow steadily, attract demand and help position you for long-term financial security.

Minimise land tax

You can buy as many properties as you can finance but, with the exception of your PPOR, you'll have to pay land tax on them.

Many people don't realise this, but each state has different land-tax thresholds and, depending on a state's regulations, just one investment property might put you above that threshold. The figure is based on unimproved land value.

For example, the land-tax threshold in Queensland is currently \$600 000, based on the unimproved land value. In New South Wales it's \$1 075 000 and in Victoria it's just \$50 000. Understanding these thresholds allows you to minimise your overall tax bill by buying properties that attract less tax.

Let's say you were to buy two \$600 000 properties in Queensland. Since the land value of each property is likely to be less than \$300 000, you could buy those properties and still be under Queensland's $600 000 threshold.

However, buying a third property in Queensland would push you over that state's land-tax threshold, so a better strategy would be to buy that property in New South Wales. You'd probably be able to buy three regional properties in that state without crossing NSW's $1 milllion-plus threshold.

Avoiding paying land tax is a strategy that keeps your tax bill down and your cash flow up. Once you own a lot of properties you are likely to have to pay land tax, but avoiding it for as long as you can will be good for your bottom line.

Be aware, too, that land-tax thresholds apply differently to properties bought through trust structures than they do to those bought under personal names. Information on this can be sourced from your office of state revenue or equivalent in your state.

Cool suburbs can achieve good long-term growth

- **Brunswick (VIC):** Once gritty but now home to coffee roasters, yoga studios and vegan eateries, this suburb has seen sharp property price growth.
- **Newtown (NSW):** Known for its bohemian vibe and thriving food scene, Newtown has become a magnet for those who value lifestyle and culture.
- **Paddington (QLD):** Property values have soared along with café culture in this historic suburb that's evolved into a brunch-lover's paradise.

How AI is reshaping due diligence in Australia

Artificial intelligence has a number of practical applications for Australian property investors, though its use is not without risk.

Here are four key ways AI can add value to your due diligence checks, and some warnings of what to watch out for.

Where AI adds real value

AI tools can effectively crunch huge volumes of data. They can compare historical sales data, rental yields, vacancy rates, even upcoming infrastructure projects across thousands of suburbs at once. They can highlight patterns a human search might miss. For example, an AI tool might spot that a specific suburb's vacancy rate has dropped for six consecutive quarters while rental prices there are climbing—a sign of strong tenant demand. Or it might identify early areas where new shopping centres, schools, roads or train stations are planned, predicting future growth.

The danger of blindly trusting AI

AI is only as good as the data it's fed. If the data is out of date or doesn't include local context, its predictions may be way off. AI may not know the local council just changed zoning laws in a specific suburb or a major employer is about to shut down in that area or the house you're looking at backs onto a noisy pub or a large construction site that could depress prices and rental returns for years. I've seen investors burned by trusting to algorithms that looked great on paper while failing to take into account human judgement and boots-on-the-ground research.

The role of human insight

This is where human insight comes in. AI can give you a shortlist of properties with potential in up-and-coming areas, but you still need a human to validate that shortlist. That means researching and visiting the area, inspecting likely properties, understanding those markets and learning all you can about property generally, including how to negotiate. Property investing isn't just about data; it's about psychology, and timing. If you outsource all your research to AI, you risk overpaying, missing red flags or buying in an area that doesn't suit your long-term goals.

The smart way to use AI for property investment

The best investors use AI as an assistant. Let the tech do the heavy lifting—to filter out poorly performing suburbs, analyse rental yields, run growth projections—but make the final decisions yourself with the aid of a trusted human expert. So think of AI as a research assistant rather than as a replacement for you as a strategist. Combine data-driven insights with expert knowledge and advice to get the best results.

To sum up, yes, AI is changing the property game but at this stage it can't (and shouldn't) replace strategy, experience and sound judgement.

Analyse the data but trust your senses

The best investors don't just analyse properties; they experience them. When I inspect a property, I use my own senses to make smarter buying decisions, to avoid expensive surprises and to choose properties tenants will love. Your senses can reveal problems a building report might miss or opportunities that have yet to make it onto the market's radar.

Most investors focus on such data as rental yield, capital growth, maintenance costs and depreciation. Those things are vitally important, but behind every data point is an actual house and if you don't draw on your senses during an inspection, you risk missing what the numbers can't tell you.

Sight

What you can see might save you thousands. Look for water damage, mould, rotting timber, structural cracks or signs of dodgy renovation. Check the roof line, look for patch jobs on gutters or fence lines. Signs of termites, like mud trails or timber shavings, can often be spotted visually.

Of course, no matter how good your eyesight, always get a building and pest report. They cost a few hundred dollars, but if issues come up, you can use them to negotiate thousands off the purchase price.

Hearing

Listen to what the agent doesn't say. Noise can ruin a great-looking investment. Stand outside the property at different times of the day and night. Can you hear traffic, trains or planes, loud music, pub or party noise, a persistently barking dog or rowdy schoolkids?

Construction sounds might signify growth—or headaches. Find out whether noise is caused by a temporary and ultimately beneficial project like a hospital or school upgrade, or whether a multi-storey apartment block or road-widening project nearby could reduce the property's value.

What you hear matters because properties with noise problems tend to have high tenant turnover, longer periods of vacancy and slower capital growth.

Touch

Touch is underrated when doing property inspections. Open windows and doors to check whether they stick. That could signal poor insulation or shifting foundations. Run your hands along the walls. Do they feel cold or damp?

Feel under sinks and behind toilets – dampness or soft cabinetry could mean hidden leaks. Bouncy or uneven boards can signal subfloor issues. Check the temperature. Is the house likely to be freezing in winter and/or very hot in summer? In places like Queensland, no air conditioning spells trouble. In colder states, a lack of proper heating is a dealbreaker for most tenants.

Smell

Sometimes you can't see mould but you can smell it. Musty smells in bathrooms, under sinks or inside wardrobes point to poor ventilation or rising damp. Strong air fresheners in every room could be masking smoke damage or pet odours soaked into carpets and, believe me, such odours can be near-impossible to get rid of.

These aren't just annoyances. They can cost thousands to remediate and if not addressed, could drive tenants away.

Taste

No, I don't lick the walls—I'm speaking metaphorically here. By taste, I mean getting the flavour of the suburb. Is the area filled with quality cafés, markets, wine bars, boutiques? Such lifestyle markers attract high-quality tenants and push rents up. As noted, suburbs like Brunswick in Melbourne, Newtown in Sydney and Paddington in Brisbane have exploded in value because of their walkability and food culture.

If you get a good vibe from the street or suburb, chances are tenants will too.

The risks of ignoring your senses

Here's what happens when you ignore your senses. You buy a beautiful-looking property but it has termite damage. You chase yield but your tenant leaves because they can't get out of their driveway thanks to traffic. You skip the in-person inspection and discover the rising damp only after settlement.

Data tells you where to buy. Your senses tell you what you might be buying.

How to inspect a property like a pro

1. Use your senses. Don't just look; experience the home. Visit at different times of day, especially in the evenings and weekends.
2. Even if everything looks fine, be sure to get a building and pest report.
3. Walk the neighbourhood, grab a coffee and feel the energy of the area.
4. Compare what you feel with what the data says. It's combining that information that leads to smart investments.

A client was about to buy a high-yield property that looked perfect on paper, but when we visited, our senses told us something wasn't right.

The agent had lit candles and turned on music, but it didn't mask the issues. The place backed onto a loud industrial site with trucks reversing in and out all day. Inside, we found damp under the sink and soft floorboards.

So we walked away and helped the client buy a quieter, cleaner property two streets over that is now tenanted and producing higher rent than the first property could have.

Reports are a great start, but your senses don't lie.

By integrating sensory observations with objective data and professional inspections, you'll position yourself better to choose a property that will not only appreciate in value but attract and retain quality tenants.

Vacancy rates are key

One of the most important things you need to look at when considering any investment property is vacancy rates.

A vacancy rate is low when nearly all rental properties are rented. A couple of years ago a rate of 3 per cent was considered equilibrium, but as rental markets have become tighter, low vacancy would probably be judged as anything below 2 per cent.

Rental vacancies are probably the first thing to look at. You don't want to buy in a suburb that has, say, a 5 or 6 per cent vacancy rate.

Case study

Building financial freedom from scratch

When Spencer and Sophie came to me, they were in their mid-thirties with a six-month-old baby. They were both employed in PAYG jobs. Their total budget was $1.5 million.

Their main goal was to achieve long-term financial freedom. They wanted more flexible working arrangements so Sophie could stop working and eventually Spencer could stop being a wage slave and run his own business.

Understanding budget vs borrowing capacity

Budget is not quite the same as borrowing capacity. Their borrowing capacity was $1.2 million, but because they had $300 000 in savings their total combined budget was $1.5 million.

The strategy

To grow their freedom fund portfolio and help them achieve their goals, we needed to plan a strategy that encompassed buying a few properties, focusing on both cash flow and capital growth.

We decided to pursue a property under $750 000 first so they'd have plenty of borrowing capacity left. They wanted to purchase something that could be positively geared and would produce a decent yield in an area that was seeing growth.

Why we focused on Perth

We decided to focus on Western Australia because our research allowed us to see that market's potential. Perth property hadn't yet boomed but it was starting to move and people were starting to talk.

At the time, Perth had the highest rental yields of any capital city apart from Darwin and capital growth was coming. I thought, yeah, we'll give Perth a go.

Property 1: Ashby, WA

We found a great property in a suburb called Ashby, 20 kilometres, or 35 minutes' drive, from Perth's CBD. We secured it for $650 000, well under our agreed budget:

- *Location:* Ashby, WA, 20 kilometres from Perth's CBD
- *Property type:* modern 4-bed, 2-bath freestanding brick house
- *Land size:* almost 600 sqm
- *Purchase price:* $650 000, under the clients' $750 000 budget
- *Strategy:* High yield + growth potential.

The result

A year later, the property was valued at $811 000, affording an as-yet-unrealised equity gain of $161 000. This represented a 25 per cent gain in just 12 months.

This enabled Spencer and Sophie to purchase another property to add to their portfolio, in line with their strategy.

Property 2: Queensland (in progress)

The focus for Spencer and Sophie's next property was Queensland, where we've been seeing solid growth and strong yields.

(continued)

We're looking for an investment property with a 5 per cent yield to start, with the option to add a granny flat to turn it into a dual-income property with a potential 7.5 per cent yield. This would put Spencer and Sophie well and truly on the path to financial independence.

Interest rates vary and banks' lending and serviceability criteria change. If the criteria become less stringent, borrowing capacity goes up. If they get tougher, borrowing capacity goes down.

The long-term plan

It's a great start, but it's not going to set them up for life. Their goal is to buy six properties, or 10 — whatever it takes.

Initially, you might look at this couple's borrowing capacity and think they'll stick with that strategy. But times change. Spencer and Sophie's borrowing capacity might increase. We might sell one of their properties to free up some debt so they can buy another property. We'll keep fleshing out the strategy.

Time and health: what really matters

Everyone with a mortgage knows it can be a lot like saving for a freedom fund — it's a trade-off.

Many couples have two incomes, so they're both working full-time to pay down the mortgage and if they've started a family, they're not seeing much of their kids. And of course, there's another level of pressure since childcare is expensive and rebates are means-tested. The trade-off can be tricky since if the mortgage is large one partner's income may be devoted to childcare costs because they earn too much to qualify for the rebate.

It's okay to say no: prioritising financial goals

It is really about lifestyle so if you do have a mortgage, it's okay to say, 'I can't do *x*, *y* or *z*—I've got a mortgage.' Maybe you can't afford to go out for dinner on a particular occasion because you're paying off a property and you can't do both. So *just say no.* Stand up for what you're trying to do.

Remember: *smart saving is about finding more cost-effective ways to do the things you don't want to give up.* If you love sharing food with friends and loved ones, don't stop socialising. Instead of eating out, invite people to your place for dinner. If you've got kids, meet up at the park for fish and chips or plan a picnic. Take turns hosting your relatives or friends for weekly or monthly catch-ups, where everyone brings a plate.

If you entertain at home and order takeaway rather than going out, it will cost you (and your loved ones) less.

The same goes for other costly pastimes:

- Host at-home movie nights where you pop your own popcorn rather than paying for movie tickets and overpriced cinema snacks.
- Take the kids to the beach rather than to an expensive water park.
- Build a home bar, bottle by bottle, and get together at home instead of spending big on Friday-night drinks.

- Organise a fun clothes swap with friends rather than blowing the budget on shopping sprees.
- Have fun making your own Christmas treats, cards and gifts.
- Grow your own herbs and veggies.
- Individually, these may seem like insignificant savings. But over time small amounts really add up.

Build your equity

Remember you don't have to save a deposit for each purchase. There are other ways to amass the funds you need to get into your next property. One way is through *building equity in your first property.*

Building equity through organic growth is important, so capital growth in that first property is one of the best ways to help you acquire your next property.

For some people a strategy focused on *creating equity*, such as renovating a well-located fixer-upper or maximising your returns by building a dual-income property, will be key. For detailed strategies on dual-income and duplex investments please refer to my book *Positively Geared, 2nd edition.*

Case study

A nurse takes control of her future

Emily came to me in her thirties. She owned no property but she had a very clear motivation. Her dad had died from cancer but her parents hadn't set things up very well and he left her mum with very little — a few thousand in the bank, no security. They were virtually living on the breadline.

The wake-up call

This happens more often than you might think. Parents work hard all their lives but retire without a nest egg in the form of property or other assets. And their kids don't want to end up there.

Watching her mum struggle after her dad died motivated Emily to take control of her future by taking steps to set herself up for financial freedom down the track.

Emily's starting position

Emily lives in Sydney, close to her mother. She has enough saved for her initial deposit. Her goal isn't to retire early or to become a property multi-millionaire or to own 10 properties in 10 years. She wants to set herself up for the future, and for her that might mean buying two properties or three.

The right property

We found Emily a dual-income property in Brisbane: a house with an attached granny flat. This property was on the market for $780 000 and, fortunately for Emily as it turned out, had been on the market for quite some time.

Properties create the most excitement when they're first listed. Typically, the longer a property stays on the market, the less interest it attracts.

The beauty of a granny flat

If your goal is financial freedom through property investing, it's crucial you think beyond a buying and holding strategy. Depending on where you buy, that strategy might work.

(continued)

If budget constraints mean you are buying into a slower-growth market — perhaps in a regional area — you might choose a property whose value could be boosted with a renovation, or one that could be made to generate extra rental income with the addition of a granny flat.

While a granny flat may not add a great deal of equity, it's a great way to transform a single-dwelling property into a dual-income, positively geared asset. And building a granny flat costs far less than building an entire house. If this strategy appeals to you, look out for a house on a block large enough to accommodate an addition and check that it meets council requirements. For example, to be compliant, you'll need a suitable access handle — enough space between any existing buildings and boundary fences to allow the building of an access driveway to service the granny flat.

How we secured the deal for Emily

I rang the agent and asked lots of questions. Agents tend to be more transparent with a buyer's agent than with someone from the general public, and in this case he gave me information he probably shouldn't have: 'Well, it was under contract but the buyer pulled out and now it's sitting there. But if you want to make us an offer, the vendors are keen to sell because they've signed a contract on another property. They have to sell it.'

I thought, 'Bingo! I'll get this property really cheap.'

Doing due diligence

We did our due diligence and everything checked out well. No termites. Not in a flood zone. Good street location. And the desperate vendors were keen to make a deal at almost any price.

We started putting in offers. The property was listed at $780 000 and in the end we bought it for $690 000. Such a low price was almost unheard of in that location at the time.

The result

By buying a languishing property, we made a massive saving:

- *Purchase price:* $690 000 (original asking price $780 000)
- *Rental income:* $815 per week
- *Yield:* 6.1 per cent
- *Property type:* house with attached granny flat (dual income)
- *Location:* Brisbane
- *Market value:* estimated to be around $800 000 given that similar properties were selling for more than $800 000
- *Instant equity:* approximately $110 000.

That's the sort of value-add we try to achieve for all our clients. Emily's equity increased instantly from the discount alone — what she *didn't* pay became equity.

Why Brisbane was the right market

Brisbane has been one of the strongest-performing property markets in Australia over the past decade. At the time we bought Emily's property, the fundamentals were exceptional:

- *Median house price in the area:* $795 000
- *Quarterly growth:* almost 4 per cent
- *12-month growth:* 13.57 per cent

(continued)

- *10-year average annual growth:* 16.22 per cent
- *Five-year population growth:* 16.4 per cent.

By late 2025, Brisbane's median house price had topped $1.1 million, with some reports placing it closer to $1.13 million. It is now the second-highest median-house-value market in Australia, having overtaken Melbourne and Canberra. The property we helped Emily buy is outperforming the average investment significantly (see figure 8.1).

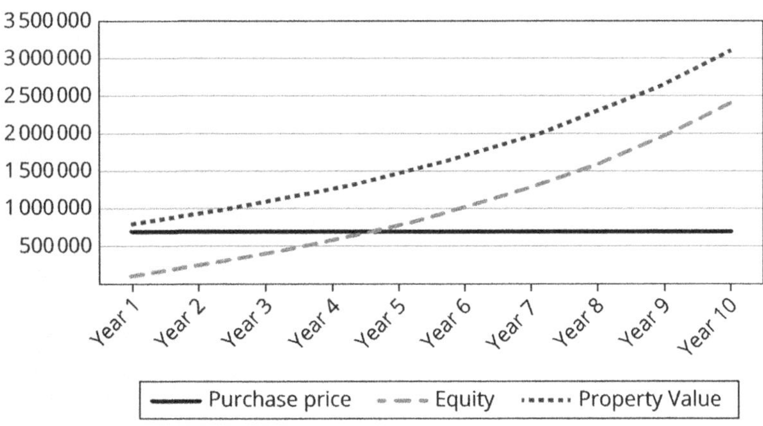

Figure 8.1 ***Emily's equity strategy***

***Using 10-year average annual growth rate 16.22%**

Source: © Commonwealth of Australia

Setting Emily up for her next purchase

When the banks assess Emily's borrowing capacity for her next purchase, she'll look great on paper because her first investment property ticks all the boxes. She purchased it under budget, 6.1 per cent yield is exceptional and it produced instant equity.

Next steps

The plan is for Emily to do a duplex development next. She'll borrow against the equity in her Brisbane property and we're considering development finance and different structures with different lenders. This duplex development will create additional equity and set her up even better for the future.

Key takeaways

- Using equity to acquire assets that generate cash flow and growth accelerates your freedom fund.
- Your goal is to build a portfolio that supports your freedom fund by balancing growth, income, risk and lifestyle goals over the long term.
- Investing in a range of types of property across a range of locations spreads your risk by reducing your exposure to localised market downturns.
- AI is changing the property game but it can't (and shouldn't) replace strategy, experience and sound judgement.

Chapter 9

Invest through a self-managed super fund

More and more Australians are looking at their superannuation balances and asking themselves, 'Could I do more with this money?' For those who like having more control, and who favour strategic asset structuring, investing through a self-managed super fund, or SMSF, means you can leverage any gains property makes in a tax-advantaged environment. But this structure does come with some restrictions, and it's not for everyone.

Use super to buy property (without getting burned by the rules)

I recently had a client who came to me because he knew of me… maybe he'd followed me on social media or read my books. He explained he had terminal cancer and had been given 12 months to live. He was trying to set up his family by buying into an SMSF. I wanted to help so I referred him to a financial planner.

But there were issues around that. The financial planner was not comfortable recommending this course of action knowing the guy was going to die, and it's extremely difficult for me to buy a property for someone in an SMSF without an adviser's recommendation. It can be done and it's legal, but there are strict conditions of compliance as well as the sole purpose test.

It was a distressing situation as well as a minefield but he trusted me, and that was humbling. I want you to avoid all that by knowing as much as possible, so here we go.

All that cash

Superannuation was once something people forgot about until they turned 65, but these days investors are proactive earlier and some are really making their super money work for them. If you want to take charge of your financial future, with property investment as a cornerstone strategy, SMSFs can be really useful.

Our SMSF sector is enormous. The Australian Taxation Office (ATO) revealed that Australians' total estimated SMSF assets were about $1.05 trillion in June 2025 and about $1.07 trillion in September 2025. There were more than 1.2 million members in 653 000 SMSFs as at 30 June 2025. So yes, SMSFs are popular. And provided you know what you can and can't do with property investments made through an SMSF, they can be a potentially powerful tool in your future financial freedom strategy.

However, you need to know that investing in property through an SMSF is not the same as buying an investment property in your own name. Because the field is heavily regulated I'm careful about the advice I give on such investments. Be aware the upside can be great but there are a few risks. You need to do your homework.

Start by getting independent advice that's tailored to your circumstances. SMSF trustees have legal responsibilities, so you really do need solid professional guidance before taking the plunge.

Let's walk through the process of SMSF property investing in a way that's clear, structured and practical so if you think it's for you, you'll be in a position to seek appropriate advice.

The right advice: who should you consult about SMSF investing?

While a buyer's agent can help you with the property purchase itself, the person who can best help you decide whether investing through an SMSF suits your circumstances, mindset and goals is a licensed financial adviser.

If you don't already have an SMSF set up, see a financial adviser with an Australian Financial Services Licence (AFSL) or a qualified accountant who's licensed to give financial advice and they will help you set one up.

This expert will also advise whether an SMSF investing strategy is likely to suit your needs. That will probably involve their drafting a Statement of Advice (SOA) confirming that the strategy fits within your broader financial plan. Once that foundation is in place, the property search can begin.

So, if a potential client comes to me and says they want to buy an SMSF property, I'll say, 'I can help you with that, but first you need to go get your SMSF and SOA set up by a qualified adviser.' If they have an SMSF in place, I'll refer them to an adviser who'll become part of their dream team so they can get that SOA set up.

But if that investor asks, 'Is it a good idea for me to buy property within my super fund?', I can't advise them. It's not that it's especially complicated; it's about compliance. If someone asks me for tax advice, I can't give it to them. I may know the answer, but I'm not a tax accountant. For similar reasons, I can't advise someone to buy an SMSF investment property. But someone can come to me once they've received advice from an appropriate adviser on buying an SMSF property, I can help them find a property that suits their strategy and situation.

Who's best suited to investing through an SMSF?

Not everyone is eligible to use an SMSF to buy property, and not everyone *should* do it even if technically they can.

SMSF property investing works best for a certain type of person. Typically, that's someone who:

- has a substantial super balance
- is comfortable with a bit of complexity
- is prepared to treat the SMSF like a regulated investment vehicle rather than as a personal finance shortcut.

The first group this strategy might suit is *people with a high enough super balance for the structure to make sense.* Around $250 000 to $300 000 is often touted as the 'ballpark minimum' to ensure SMSF property investing is cost-effective. It's not a legally required minimum balance so much as a reality check, because there are fixed costs that come with running an SMSF. There are also higher deposits and lower loan-to-value ratios (LVRs) for properties purchased in an SMSF. Self-managing your super involves administration, annual audits, tax returns and often specialist support. If the balance isn't sufficiently high, those costs take a comparatively bigger bite out of your fund, and the strategy can become inefficient.

The reality is that SMSF property investing is probably not the ideal strategy for first-time investors. You certainly don't want to be figuring it out as you go when it comes to, say, compliance. The rules are not flexible.

An experienced investor might want to consider buying property through an SMSF. If you already understand property fundamentals and you're prepared to bone up on SMSF rules and regulations, you'll be well placed to succeed.

A business owner might want to invest through an SMSF, particularly when investing in commercial property. There are scenarios in which an SMSF can acquire business real estate then lease it back to a related-party business, provided it's done at market value and is documented correctly. This can be a useful strategy when it also aligns with your business and retirement plans, and when compliance requirements are respected.

It's not for everyone

I also want to be clear about who might want to *reconsider* whether to invest through an SMSF.

If your balance is below that 'rough cost-effectiveness' threshold of $250 000 to $300 000, the SMSF structure can become top-heavy.

There are ongoing management costs such as extra accounting and compliance fees that can have a negative impact on your returns if the fund is too small.

You may also end up buying a poor property because that's all the fund can afford—and then the fund becomes undiversified and cash-poor.

If you might want quick access to cash, I'd advise against investing in property through your SMSF. That's because if you buy a property in this way, any rental income stays inside the super fund, which means you can't access it as you can personal income. Superannuation has preservation rules and conditions around release of funds held within it. Property inside an SMSF is designed to support your retirement, not to fund lifestyle spending today.

Note too that not all banks are willing to lend money for SMSF property purchases. This can limit your options and make the terms of settlement less flexible than those for conventional property loans.

Another consideration is that SMSF property investing involves ongoing work. Sure, you can outsource parts of it, but the ultimate responsibility lies with you.

What if all I have is $300 000 in super and no savings?

I buy a lot of properties for SMSF clients who may not have a lot of savings but do have a lot of super. This makes them a fit for an SMSF strategy, but most of our clients buy both inside and outside of SMSFs. If you have minimal or no savings but can get yourself set up with an SMSF, do so but only if your experienced financial adviser supports that decision as aligned with your wealth-creation strategy.

Personally, I've preferred putting more money into property than into super because from what I've seen, the capital growth in property has been better. But again, it's a personal thing. You might speak to a financial adviser who recommends super because it's taxed a lot more leniently than property investments.

Around $300 000 in superannuation is typically the minimum required to make an SMSF property purchase feasible. In practice, though, thanks to lending restrictions on super funds, you might need more. Financial institutions are generally more conservative when it comes to SMSF lending, usually requiring a deposit of around 40 per cent. So the amount you hold in super directly impacts your borrowing power and overall investment strategy.

The SMSF purchasing process

The biggest misconception about buying property through an SMSF is that it works like a normal purchase but with a different source of deposit money. That's not the case.

An SMSF property purchase is constrained, particularly around borrowing, cash flow and what expenses can be paid from where. Nonetheless buying property through your SMSF does have benefits over buying outside of it. Because the fund is its own entity, it also has its own borrowing capacity.

If you earn, say, $100 000 a year, that'll get you a certain borrowing capacity. But once you've maxed that out, you can still buy property through an SMSF. The amount you can borrow will be based on how much you have in super, irrespective of your income. Because super isn't part of your income, the bank assesses it differently. Any income from the property you buy through an SMSF goes into a super-fund loan that you have to pay down in the same way as you must pay down any loan.

When you buy property in a super fund, there are certain rules. For instance, you cannot develop, renovate or subdivide that property. It's a 'set-and-forget' purchase. You're buying it for cash flow and capital growth.

Step 1: Establish an SMSF

The first step in buying property through a super fund is establishing an SMSF—or, if you already have one, ensuring it has been established correctly. Check that:

- the fund is set up properly
- its deed allows for property investment
- trustees are in place
- the fund has an investment strategy that supports the decision to purchase property through it. The investment strategy is not a formality; it's part of demonstrating that the decisions made with regard to that SMSF align with the fund's purpose.

Step 2: Make a limited recourse borrowing arrangement

If the fund is going to borrow, it will usually do so through a Limited Recourse Borrowing Arrangement, or LRBA. This is a special type of borrowing in which the lender's rights are generally limited to the asset acquired under the arrangement. It exists because SMSFs are otherwise heavily restricted from borrowing. The ATO explains LRBAs and the rules for entering them, and it's important to read their guidelines given borrowing inside super is not normal lending.

Step 3: Manage property within an SMSF

Once you've acquired a property through an SMSF, all costs associated with it, including mortgage payments, rates, insurance, repairs and property management fees, must be paid from that SMSF. You cannot cover an expense from your personal account, however convenient that might be. That is one of the reasons liquidity planning matters. Your SMSF must be able to stand on its own feet.

Can you use your SMSF to buy your own home or business premises?

SMSF property is heavily shaped by restrictions that exist to stop people using super as a vehicle for personal benefit pre-retirement. So SMSF property investment is strictly for investment purposes.

Any property bought through a super fund must meet the sole-purpose test, which ensures that any assets within the SMSF exist solely to provide benefits in retirement, not personal benefits today. The Australian Government website Moneysmart is clear that such property must not be lived in—or rented to—fund members or related parties. There's no way around this. Your SMSF can acquire residential property as an investment, but that property cannot be dealt with either by you or by your family. You can't live in it. You can't rent it to yourself. You can't rent it to relatives. You can't treat it as a holiday home even if you only use it occasionally.

Commercial property is different in one key way. There are circumstances in which the SMSF can lease commercial premises to a related business, provided it does so at market value, everything is documented properly and the rent is paid on time, in full, with no casual arrangements.

That is why SMSF commercial property is often attractive to business owners: it can turn rent into an internal wealth-building mechanism. Because if you then lease that property to your business, you can pay rent into your own retirement fund instead of to a third party. But all must be above board and always satisfy the sole purpose principle.

The same investment-purpose rules apply to rural and industrial property.

There are further restrictions around property renovations and development. SMSF borrowing structures are not designed for speculative development or for flipping properties. If an LRBA is in place, there will be limitations around improvements. You should get specialist advice before assuming you can get a return on a renovator's delight through your SMSF. Generally, you can't buy a property through an SMSF and materially alter it to manufacture value. Subdividing, developing or building multiple dwellings on a property purchased as a single dwelling are usually not permitted, particularly if borrowing structures such as LRBAs are involved.

There's a legal grey area between repairs and improvements but even the most basic renovations of properties held by SMSFs should only be undertaken with professional advice. Minor updates to a property, such as maintenance or cosmetic work, may be possible if these works are paid from the SMSF itself but, broadly speaking, significant renovations or development-style projects won't fit within the structure.

To summarise the rules applying to SMSFs:

- A fund must have at least one member and a maximum of six.
- If the trustees of the fund are individuals, each member of the fund must be a trustee. If the trustee of the fund is a company, each member of the fund must be a director of the company. Trustees cannot receive remuneration for their trustee services from the SMSF.
- As a trustee you are required to prepare and implement an investment strategy for your SMSF and to review it regularly.
- As the trustee of an SMSF you are required each year to lodge audited financials and tax returns with the ATO as the regulator governing SMSFs. You must ensure all assets are properly valued at 30 June each year.
- As I've noted, under no circumstances may you withdraw money from your SMSF prior to reaching a condition of release, normally retirement. The penalties are very, very severe.
- This also means you cannot use the property in the SMSF as your own home or as your personal holiday home.

What type of properties best suit SMSF investors?

Because of these limitations, experienced SMSF investors typically focus on acquiring set-and-manage-carefully properties that will perform well over the long term. This generally means houses that either are relatively new or have been well renovated and are situated in growth locations offering reliable rental yield.

Since any asset held in an SMSF is intended to support your retirement, risk management becomes even more important. So look to buy a property you're confident will perform without needing major intervention.

The takeaway message here is this: if you're keen to enjoy the tax benefits of SMSF property investing, do your research, work with experts and if in doubt, don't just forge ahead: consult the financial adviser and accountant on your dream team.

Case study

Building $250 000 passive income in 15 years

James and Sarah are long-term clients who have been proactive investors for years. They'd already started searching for their next acquisition before we met for a strategy session. The focus was stepping back and looking at the bigger picture. We analysed the likely impact of their next purchase and mapped out a broad strategy.

Their target is ambitious: within 15 years, they want to reach a point where they're bringing in $250 000 a year in passive income to sustain the lifestyle they're working toward. That's high — most clients aim for somewhere between $100 000 and $150 000. But every strategy starts with the client's goals, and that's what we built the plan around.

James and Sarah's current portfolio position

They hold three properties: an owner-occupier in Rosebery, Sydney, an investment property in Brown Street, Paddington, valued at around $690 000 with comparable sales pushing above $700 000, and another in Albury, purchased in 2024 and already showing solid growth.

Overall, their portfolio's LVR sits at around 50 per cent. The Brown Street property alone has amassed roughly $350 000 in equity since they bought it, with around $200 000 of that borrowable. Across the portfolio, they're sitting on close to $1 million in potential borrowable equity, assuming an 80 per cent LVR.

Adjusting the timeline

Originally, their plan was based on a 21-year horizon, with an inflation-adjusted passive income goal of around $420 000 a year. James wants to bring that timeline forward to 15 years, which necessitated a more aggressive acquisition and debt strategy.

The upside is that inflation has less time to compound, so the equivalent target drops to around $360 000 in future dollars — still ambitious but achievable with the right structure in place.

The next acquisition

James and Sarah are now targeting another purchase at around the $620 000 mark. The modelling assumes a rental yield of around 4.75 per cent, 5 per cent long-term growth (conservative) and funding from equity in their Sydney property on a principal-and-interest loan.

Because interest rates are currently higher than the projected rental yield from their portfolio, their proposed purchase will have a slight negative impact on cash flow in the short term.

(continued)

This reinforces the message that a single acquisition won't enable them to achieve their passive-income goal. Each property purchase is part of a staged portfolio build.

James and Sarah's SMSF strategy

A major component of James and Sarah's strategy is a self-managed super fund. The plan involves purchasing a residential SMSF property in 2027 for roughly $850 000, holding it for about 10 years, then selling it and redeploying the capital into commercial property.

Projections suggest the re-sale of that property in 2037 would net them around $1.5 million, leaving them roughly $1.6 million in super after tax. Their plan is to reinvest that money in a commercial asset valued at around $2 million, with a stronger yield.

Once the debt on it is reduced, that commercial property alone could generate close to $188 000 annually, becoming the cornerstone of James and Sarah's passive-income strategy.

Managing borrowing capacity

Borrowing capacity will likely be a limiting factor for James and Sarah as their portfolio grows. Debt recycling will help them restructure their debt into a more tax-deductible form without increasing their overall exposure to risk. This will involve paying down the mortgage on the owner-occupier property then reborrowing for investment.

We discussed the pros and cons of opting for interest-only lending on investment properties to improve cash flow and allow them to pay down their non-deductible home-loan debt faster.

Two investment pathways

We modelled two main scenarios.

The first involves fewer acquisitions, with a major debt reduction phase around 2042, potentially delivering more than $475 000 a year in passive income by around 2043.

The second includes additional acquisitions and produces stronger early cash flow, meaning they'd reach their passive-income target slightly later, around 2044.

Both approaches would work. The decision would come down to the couple's risk tolerance, timing preference and cash-flow comfort.

The outcome

James and Sarah are already in a strong position, with equity, experience and a clear long-term vision. Their passive-income target is at the higher end but it's achievable provided they make disciplined acquisitions, use their SMSF strategically and manage debt carefully.

The planned sell-down of their first SMSF investment property and reinvestment into commercial property will likely be the key accelerant in their strategy, transforming a solid residential portfolio into a lifestyle-supporting passive-income base.

James and Sarah's freedom strategy in a nutshell

- Existing Sydney home plus two investment properties
- Around 50 per cent portfolio LVR with ~$1 million borrowable equity

(continued)

- Passive-income target: $250 000 annually within 15 years
- Next acquisition: residential property valued at around $620 000, funded via equity
- SMSF residential purchase targeted for 2027
- Planned sale of SMSF residential property to fund ~$2 million in commercial property
- Debt recycling to preserve borrowing capacity
- Interest-only lending to optimise cash flow
- Strategy tracking toward meeting their passive-income milestone by about 2043–44.

The pros and cons: is buying through your SMSF worth it?

One of the big reasons people consider buying property through an SMSF is the difference in tax treatment. In broad terms, the tax rate on superannuation attracts concessions. There can also be differences between the investment rules in the accumulation and pension phases of an SMSF. The details depend on the fund's circumstances and you'll probably need specialist advice to tease out whether and when to invest through an SMSF. But the high-level appeal is real and is a common topic of discussion in SMSF property planning.

The pros

There are tax benefits associated with holding property within a self-managed super fund.

Pro 1: Tax advantages

The SMSF structure offers considerable tax advantages, including the potential for tax-free income, depending on the stage the fund is at and its members' circumstances.

Table 9.1 summarises the key tax benefits of buying an investment property inside an SMSF. The information it contains is drawn from ATO guidelines.

Table 9.1 ***comparative tax benefits of buying property inside and outside an SMSF***

Tax benefit	How it works in an SMSF	Key details/conditions
Concessional tax rate on rental income	Inside a complying SMSF, rental income is taxed at 15%.	This is significantly lower than personal marginal tax rates (up to 45%) or company tax (30%).
Capital gains tax (CGT) discount	If the property is held for 12+ months, the SMSF receives a one-third CGT discount on that property, reducing it to 10%.	Applies only in the accumulation phase.
Tax-free capital gains in pension phase	Once the SMSF is paying a retirement-phase pension, capital gains on assets supporting that pension can be tax-free.	This is part of the ATO's Exempt Current Pension Income (ECPI) rules.
Tax-free rental income in the SMSF pension phase	Rental income from assets supporting a retirement-phase pension may be tax-free.	Requires the fund to be in the retirement phase and compliant with Australian pension standards.
Deductions for property-related expenses	SMSFs can deduct many expenses related to holding and managing the property.	Tax-deductible expenses include property management fees, insurances, council rates, legal fees, repairs, maintenance and some improvements (subject to rules).

(continued)

Table 9.1 *comparative tax benefits of buying property inside and outside an SMSF (cont'd)*

Tax benefit	How it works in an SMSF	Key details/conditions
Depreciation deductions	SMSFs can claim depreciation on eligible assets (plant and equipment) and capital works.	Division 40 (depreciation) and Division 43 (capital works) apply.
Interest deductions on SMSF property loans	Interest on a Limited Recourse Borrowing Arrangement (LRBA) is deductible.	Must comply with strict LRBA rules and the loan must be for a single acquirable asset.
Concessional tax on foreign fund transfers used for property investment	If foreign superannuation is transferred into the SMSF and used for investment, the assessable portion can be taxed at 15 per cent instead of at the member's marginal rate.	Requires meeting ATO conditions for foreign fund transfers.
Ability to offset expenses against rental income	All allowable deductions reduce the SMSF's taxable income.	Helps reduce the effective tax rate further, below 15% in the accumulation phase.
CGT exemption for segregated pension assets	If the property is what's called a 'segregated pension asset', all capital gains are tax-exempt.	Applies only when the asset is fully supporting a retirement-phase pension.

Pro 2: More control over your business premises

Having greater control is another advantage of buying property through a self-managed super fund since you may choose the asset rather than relying on pooled investment decisions. For experienced and disciplined investors, such control is valuable.

For example, you can buy a commercial property through an SMSF, then lease it to yourself or to a business you're associated with, which ensures long-term stability. Leasing a property from your SMSF can create a long-term arrangement that benefits both the business and the fund, but it must be leased at market value and everything pertaining to its use must be fully documented.

Pro 3: Protection of assets

Super funds are widely viewed as a protected environment tax-wise, and asset protection is sometimes cited, particularly by business owners, as a reason for buying property through an SMSF. One plus is that, under Australian law, if your SMSF-held property falls over and you default on the loan, the lender can seize only that asset; everything else in the SMSF is protected.

The cons

Now for the disadvantages.

Con 1: Lack of liquidity

This is probably the biggest risk because property is, by its large and chunky nature, an illiquid asset. If your SMSF needs cash to pay property-related expenses, compensate for vacancies, comply with audits or, eventually, make member payments in retirement, property may not always cooperate. This is why *diversification matters* and why a fund that becomes all property and no cash can be a sticky trap.

Con 2: Conditions on borrowing

Borrowing through SMSFs is typically more expensive and restrictive than it is for individuals. The Limited Recourse Borrowing Arrangement (LRBA) you make to secure a loan for an SMSF acquisition is not like a normal loan: it can carry higher interest rates, require a larger deposit and allow less flexibility than personal lending. ATO guidance makes clear that SMSF borrowing is permitted only in limited circumstances, and associated LRBAs come with specific compliance conditions.

Con 3: Compliance requirements

The strict compliance rules can be burdensome (table 9.2). SMSFs require annual audits, administration, record-keeping and ongoing attention. Even if you outsource tasks, as trustee you are still responsible.

Table 9.2 ***risk and compliance (complements the tax benefits)***

Risk/issue	Description	Why it matters
Liquidity risk	Property ties up a large portion of the SMSF's assets.	The SMSF must always meet pension payments, expenses and loan obligations.
Borrowing restrictions (LRBA)	Only limited-recourse loans are allowed. Strict rules on repairs versus improvements apply.	Non-compliance can invalidate deductions or breach super law.
Related-party restrictions	Residential property cannot be rented to members or to relatives.	A breach risks fund non-compliance.
Concentration risk	One property may dominate the SMSF portfolio.	This reduces your ability to diversify and increases your exposure to market downturns.
Valuation and audit requirements	Annual valuations and independent audits are required.	This adds both cost and administrative complexity.
Changing legislation	Superannuation rules can change.	Long-term strategies must account for regulatory risk.

Key considerations for compliance

- Does your SMSF property purchase pass the sole purpose test? Property acquired through an SMSF must be held solely to provide retirement benefits.
- Can you ensure the property will not be for personal use? Neither SMSF members nor related parties can live in or rent an SMSF-held property unless it is a commercial property leased at market rates.
- Does your proposed SMSF property purchase comply with SMSF borrowing rules? LRBAs are tightly regulated and only a single acquirable asset can be purchased.
- Does the property you're considering buying through your SMSF need a few repairs or costly improvements? While repairs are deductible under SMSF property rules, improvements may need to be capitalised.

In a nutshell: should I invest through an SMSF?

First check to ensure this strategy suits your situation. Does it fulfil a real need, suit your way of working and align with your long-term goals? In my view, SMSF property investing works best when:

- it is part of a coherent retirement plan
- the fund has enough scale and liquidity
- the people involved are willing to respect the structure.

Here's how to avoid some of the most common mistakes investors make when using this strategy.

Mistake 1: Starting with insufficient super

Start with your super balance. While there's no strict minimum, unless the balance is comfortably into six figures, ongoing costs can outweigh the benefits. If you buy a less-than-ideal property because it's all you can afford, the fund becomes undiversified and cash flow is likely to be tight. If you're going to work the SMSF property strategy to your advantage, you must build in scale and breathing room.

The commonly cited baseline of $250 000 to $300 000 in superannuation before you purchase substantial assets like property to bolster your SMSF is not a legal threshold, but it's a good rule of thumb.

Mistake 2: Failing to budget for ongoing expenses

Loan repayments, property costs, accounting and audit fees, and compliance administration are all expenses that must be paid from the SMSF year in, year out. If you don't build these into your modelling, you may end up losing ground.

Mistake 3: Failing to comply with the rules governing SMSF assets

Investors assume common sense applies, but the SMSF rules don't operate like that. The government is explicit that to live in the property and/or rent it to related parties puts you in breach of the law.

Mistake 4: Poor planning around liquidity

Poor liquidity planning bites a lot of SMSF property investors on the bum. Your super fund must be able to pay fund-related bills, withstand vacancies and, eventually, support retirement payments.

If the SMSF is concentrated in a single illiquid asset, no matter how valuable that asset may be, juggling costs may still result in month-to-month stress.

Mistake 5: Viewing SMSF-held property as passive

Property invested through SMSFs is often mistakenly viewed as passive when in reality running an SMSF requires the owner's active oversight, even if professionals are involved. If you'd prefer to avoid that responsibility, I strongly advise against this structure.

If you understand the responsibilities and the investment clearly supports your long-term retirement goals, it may be worth exploring further.

Is an SMSF investment strategy right for you?

The best way to think about SMSF property is to *remove emotion and focus on fit.*

If you have a decent super balance, if you understand property, if you're prepared to handle complex compliance requirements and if this investment strategy supports your retirement plan, it is certainly viable.

But if your aim is to use super as a workaround to enable you to buy a lifestyle property or if you need the rental income personally or if the fund will be stretched thin after the proposed property purchase, it is probably the wrong move for you.

SMSF-held property is a powerful tool to have in your box because it allows you to take back control of your super and think long term. But you need to approach it with some caution.

My advice is that you build the right team around you. Make sure your accountant, mortgage broker and SMSF specialist are aligned—and on speed dial. And make sure you understand what you are buying and why because the goal isn't to own property within super as a trophy. The goal is to build retirement security in a way that works.

Whether or not you choose to pursue an SMSF investment strategy, at this stage you may well be looking to unlock some of your equity through downsizing, diversifying and optimizing your portfolio, which is the subject of the next chapter.

Key takeaways

- Investing through a self-managed super fund, or SMSF, means you can leverage any gains property makes in a tax-advantaged environment.
- If you have a sufficient super balance, understand property and are prepared to handle complex compliance requirements, and if this investment strategy supports your retirement plan, it may be worth exploring further.
- Property inside an SMSF is designed to support your retirement, not to fund lifestyle spending today.
- If you're keen to enjoy the tax benefits of SMSF property investing, do your research, work with experts and consult a financial adviser and accountant.

Chapter 10

Downsize and diversify for retirement

As you reach your retirement years, you may be thinking less about getting that home on the water and more about getting into a position that's more secure than the one you're in now.

Here in Australia, if you've reached your sixties there's a very good chance you've done a lot of things right. You've worked hard, raised a family and have probably bought a home along the way. And if you bought that home 20, 30 or 40 years ago, it's likely to be worth several times what you paid for it.

Depending on your circumstances, I might suggest downsizing and living off the extra money. Or downsizing and buying an investment property with the difference. If you can pay cash for that investment property, it will bring in some passive income. If the kids have moved out and you're empty nesters, that opens up more options.

What I see all the time is that people reach retirement age asset rich but cash poor. They've got significant wealth tied up in property, usually the family home, but not so much in the way of accessible income. This can be stressful because, as I explain in this chapter, retirement isn't just about what you own. It's about how you live. It's about having income, flexibility and peace of mind.

I meet a lot of people in their fifties, sixties and seventies who have assumed everything would just work itself out and that superannuation plus a paid-off home would equal financial security. Sometimes that's true, but often it isn't. Often the biggest issue is that their wealth is locked into their main asset, the property they live in.

You can live in a five-million-dollar house and still struggle financially if there's no income attached. Equity is great, but it doesn't pay for groceries, travel, medical or unexpected expenses that these days might include weather-related damage to your home that isn't covered by insurance. The solution may be to access your equity and turn it into income.

Income is what really matters

A comfortable retirement isn't about how much you own; it's about how much income you have coming in. That's where a properly structured investment property can play a really big role. Rental income can provide you with consistent cash flow and, unlike some investments, it tends to increase in value over time. Because rents generally increase in line with inflation, population growth and demand, they can be a fairly reliable income source in retirement.

As you get older, cash flow and achieving equity are both important, so you might consider investing in two streams. You might build a duplex or other small development, for example, then sell it and use the profits to pay down other debt. You've got a portfolio you're holding alongside developments you're selling to pay off the debt on what you keep.

That's why you need an exit plan. For example, you might buy twice as many properties as you want to end up with, then sell half of them to pay off the other half.

Just shifting from an asset-value to an income mindset can change your perspective. Once you start thinking about how your property can produce income rather than simply appreciate, the strategy makes sense.

The downsizing conversation

Downsizing comes up a lot once people hit their fifties and sixties, and there's a really practical reason for that. Your home may be paid off, or close to it, and its value may have grown significantly. You might be sitting on a lot of equity without necessarily having much in the way of liquid savings or income-producing assets.

You could decide to sell the family home and buy something cheaper—a townhouse, a duplex or just a smaller house that better suits your lifestyle. The big advantage is that you may well be able to buy that next property debt-free and still have a surplus that will become your retirement freedom fund.

In other words, downsizing can give people who have worked hard all their lives, but maybe haven't built big super balances or investment portfolios, a path to a secure retirement.

The next question people usually ask is whether the surplus money after downsizing should be reinvested. And the answer really depends on your individual situation, but generally I'll say you want that money to work for you. If someone ends up with, say, $1.5 million dollars after downsizing, I'll often suggest investing at least part of it.

The Porsche principle

Yes, you've worked all your life and you deserve to live well. Of course, you can sell your home and buy a Porsche, but what income will you have later on?

I'm not saying, 'Don't buy a Porsche!' I think people should enjoy life. But if you're going to forgo a comfortable lifestyle because you bought an expensive car and now you've got no money apart from the pension, that's probably not the smart thing to do.

You also don't need a new Porsche for $700 000 when you can buy a 20-year-old Porsche for $70 000. It's still a Porsche and they hold their value pretty well.

So by all means reward yourself. Just don't compromise your long-term security. That might mean buying an investment property outright so there's rental income coming in without any mortgage stress. I've got clients who've done exactly that. They downsize and use part of the surplus cash to purchase an investment property outright. The rent from that property becomes an ongoing and very reassuring income stream in retirement.

You don't need to invest all your surplus funds in property. You could put some into managed funds that pay dividends or interest. Those investments also generate income, often paid quarterly, that will help cover living expenses while the capital remains invested.

The key idea is that whatever investment path you take, the principal stays invested but produces income. That income might come from rent, dividends or interest. Either way, you're not just sitting on cash that slowly loses value to inflation. You're actually getting paid so you've got money coming in to live on.

When people hear the term *dividends* they may think of shares, and that can certainly be part of it. But often in this context we're referring to managed investment funds. Such funds invest across a range of assets and distribute profits back to investors periodically. It's not superannuation in this case; it's simply another form of investment income.

Downsizing, then, isn't just about moving to a smaller place. It's about unlocking equity. For many Australians, it's one of the simplest and most effective financial adjustments they can make in later life.

Rental income in retirement

Rental income is one of the simplest ways property can support retirement. A well-located property with good tenant demand can provide consistent income for years that can supplement super, reduce reliance on the pension and boost your financial freedom. A steady rental income can provide psychological comfort. People sleep better.

Veggies vs dessert

In property, everyone wants to talk about dessert, the exciting stuff. It's the hot spot you saw on the news, the flashy new development or the mining town that's going to boom overnight.

When we start thinking about investing it can be appealing to go out and buy a high-cash-flow property. I've done it myself, but it can be a mistake—one I don't want you to make.

Just as when you were a kid, you have to eat your veggies before you can have your dessert. In property terms, veggies are your strategy and long-term plan. They may not be the most exciting part of the process, but they are vital for a healthy retirement. When you pass 60 you can chase dessert provided you've finished your veggies.

Eating your veggies means asking the simple questions first:

- **What is my specific income goal?** Do I need $50 000 a year for a modest retirement or $150 000 so I can travel more and help the grandkids?
- **What is my risk tolerance?** Can I handle a period of vacancy or do I need a blue-chip property for which the rental demand is constant?
- **Does this fit my life stage?** A high-growth, zero-yield property might be great for a 25-year-old, but it won't pay your bills in retirement.

The danger of only eating dessert

I've seen plenty of people buy in a single-industry mining town because the rental yields look incredible.

I learned this lesson the hard way myself with my fourth property. During the boom I bought in Blackwater, a mining town in Central Queensland. I'd decided I wanted to build a positive cash flow portfolio and, as my adviser promised, Blackwater was great. The rent was $800 a week. But when the industry turned, that rent plummeted to $190 almost overnight. The property's value dropped by half. If it had been my only source of retirement income, I'd have been in serious trouble. The rent has gradually recovered over time, but it's still well below what it once achieved (it's now bringing in around $300 a week). It's negatively geared these days and, yes, that does provide some tax benefits.

I've paid off many other properties, but that one still carries debt. Frankly, I keep it partly because it's a constant reminder of what not to do.

A successful portfolio for a retiree is one in which the veggies—quality properties in diversified economies—are the foundation.

Inflation is the silent risk

Inflation is a big factor in retirement planning. Inflation hits the news when it leads to interest rate rises but it has a wider impact on the cost of living. Healthcare, insurance, food, utilities and travel costs all creep up over time, and if your income doesn't keep up your dream lifestyle may cease to be affordable.

Property can help hedge against inflation because both rents and property values tend to rise over time. The property market experiences cycles, but historically it's been a pretty solid inflation buffer. It's one reason many retirees keep some exposure to property even after downsizing.

Choose the right property later in life

The type of property you buy in your sixties might not be what you'd have bought in your thirties. As easy maintenance and accessibility become more important, many older people seek out secure, convenient, single-level homes or townhouses located close to essential amenities.

At the same time, financial stability is key. Chasing speculative investments late in life rarely makes sense. High-yield mining towns or oversupplied apartment markets can look attractive on paper but carry risks retirees don't need to take.

There are ways to get higher yields without taking big risks. Look for solid fundamentals: good locations, diverse economic drivers and strong tenant demand.

Two obvious options are a duplex, which brings in twice the rental income, or a commercial property, which typically has higher yields than residential property.

Why commercial property makes sense later in life

Once people move into their fifties and sixties, their property strategy may shift. Earlier in life they may have focused on growth, building equity and getting that asset base established. If people in their sixties are buying property it's usually part of the process of downsizing. The focus tends to move more towards income, stability and simplicity.

Among the biggest appeals of commercial property are higher yields and the fact that often tenants cover outgoings such as council rates, water rates and sometimes even land tax. All this means the net income can be stronger. A blue-chip residential property might generate a 3 to 3.5 per cent yield before accounting for maintenance, rates, insurance and property management fees. A commercial property might generate upwards of a 7 per cent yield, with all the costs covered by the tenant.

And lease structures are different. Residential tenants typically sign 12-month leases, sometimes shorter, but commercial tenants often prefer three-year, five-year or even longer lease terms. Knowing you've got a tenant locked in for several years can make cash-flow planning easier.

Another factor is borrowing capacity. By the time people reach their sixties, they've often already built up equity through residential property. They might have paid off the mortgage on their home, bought a couple of investment properties and accumulated some capital. As older investors face constraints with lending, this accumulated capital, combined with the long-term stability of commercial leases and the onus on the tenant to maintain the property, can make commercial property a more desirable and realistic choice.

While the deposits required to buy commercial premises are typically higher than for residential property, it is possible in some cases to borrow using what's known as a 'lease-doc loan'. Essentially, the lender looks primarily at the strength of the lease and the tenant's ability to pay rent rather than considering your personal income alone. It's not suitable for everyone, and you'll still need good advice, but it can open doors for investors who have solid assets but lower personal income as they transition into retirement.

Of course, higher yield comes with different risks, particularly around vacancy and tenant stability, which is why commercial property tends to work best once you've already got a solid foundation in residential. But from purely an income perspective, it's easy to see why commercial attracts people later in their lives.

But keep in mind that commercial isn't necessarily better; it's just different. It has advantages and risks. Vacancy periods can be longer. Lending can be tighter. And the type of tenant you secure becomes critical.

Commercial or residential?

I suggest investors build a solid residential base before jumping into commercial property. Some commercial specialists might disagree with me, but from a long-term perspective, residential tends to offer strong capital growth, lower vacancy risk and a bit more stability. It's usually a safer starting point.

But once you've got that foundation in place, commercial property can absolutely play a role.

Why 'residential first' makes sense

Residential property's simple advantage is that people always need somewhere to live. That fundamental demand underpins both rental stability and long-term growth. History shows a well-located residential property, particularly in an area with strong infrastructure, employment and lifestyle appeal, will generally perform well over time.

There's also the comfort factor. Most people understand residential property because they've lived in it themselves. They know what constitutes a good house, what tenants will look for, what areas feel desirable. That familiarity helps build confidence early in an investment journey.

Lending also tends to be more accessible. Banks typically require smaller deposits for residential property, often around 20 per cent and sometimes less depending on the circumstances. Commercial lending deposits are usually tighter. You might only get 70 per cent loan-to-value, sometimes less, which means you need a larger deposit upfront.

Case study

Yield vs growth for retirement income

The scenario: A couple in their early sixties have just sold their large family home in Sydney. After purchasing a smaller, single-level townhouse for cash, they have $1.5 million left to invest as their retirement nest egg. They are debating whether it's better for them to buy a high-growth blue-chip residential property or a high-yield commercial property.

Option A: Blue-chip residential property

- *Location:* established suburb in Sydney such as Dulwich Hill
- *Purchase price:* ~$1.5 million
- *Rental yield:* ~3.5 per cent ($1010 per week)
- *Gross annual income:* ~$52 500
- *Historical growth:* ~7 per cent per annum (values typically double every seven to 10 years).

Option B: High-yield commercial property

- *Location:* a regional industrial hub or retail strip
- *Purchase price:* ~$1.5 million
- *Rental yield:* ~7 per cent ($2019 per week)
- *Gross annual income:* ~$105 000
- *Historical growth:* generally lower and more volatile than blue-chip residential.

The commercial property advantage — and the catch

Commercial property really shines when it comes to income. The net return can be stronger because yields are often higher than those for residential. Further, tenants frequently pay outgoings and sometimes land tax.

But there's another side to it. If a commercial tenant does leave, vacancy periods can be significantly longer than they are for residential. Finding new people to rent a house is usually straightforward but finding a business that fits your commercial space can take months.

During any vacancy period, you'll cover all the outgoings yourself. I always ask investors to consider before they buy commercial property: 'Could I comfortably afford six months without rent if I had to?'

If the answer is no, it might be worth strengthening your residential base first.

Growth perspective: the reality

From a pure capital-growth perspective, residential property often has the edge over the long term. Commercial property certainly grows in value too, but the primary driver there is usually yield and tenant stability rather than rapid property price appreciation.

As I've discussed, residential markets are influenced by population growth, housing supply, infrastructure and lifestyle factors. Commercial property is tied to business conditions, industry trends and economic cycles. The two markets behave differently, which is why I generally view commercial as an income play to be layered on top of an existing residential portfolio, rather than as a replacement for it.

Location still matters

Location is critical in both residential and commercial property markets, but in commercial it can be even more specific. A busy road might suit some businesses perfectly but deter others. Industrial areas attract certain tenants but exclude others.

The COVID-19 pandemic highlighted this: office spaces, cafés and some retail businesses struggled when people stopped commuting and working in traditional environments. Meanwhile, medical services, logistics and essential retail often weren't affected.

All this means that when buying commercial property, it's not just about the building. It's also about the tenant profile, the surrounding business environment and how resilient that sector is likely to be in difficult times.

Lending surprises can happen

Commercial lending can be unpredictable. I've seen banks change lending policies in mid cycle. For example, an investor might secure a loan at 70 per cent loan-to-value only for the bank to later reduce its exposure and require additional equity. It doesn't happen every day, but it does happen. If it does, you'll need advice from experienced commercial brokers or advisers.

Interest rates on commercial loans tend to be slightly higher than those for residential, a factor you'll need to consider when weighing up returns.

Tenant fit-out and long-term useability

One aspect investors sometimes overlook is how tailored a space needs to be for a specific tenant. A doctor's surgery, for example, will often have a specialised fit-out but the next occupant may require significant changes. This adds another layer of risk compared with residential property as most tenants are simply looking for a comfortable home.

Due diligence becomes crucial. Ideally, you buy commercial property with an established tenant in place who has a strong lease history and a class of business that's likely to remain viable long term. But recognising whether a building could suit multiple tenant types in the future is also important, since tenants can change.

Residential headaches aren't usually what people imagine

Some investors are drawn to commercial property because they think residential investing is fraught with tenant headaches. Yes, occasionally you'll encounter a difficult tenant but choosing the right property—one in an area with strong owner-occupier appeal and high owner-occupier ratios—often correlates with stable tenants and lower turnover. And a good property manager should ensure things run smoothly.

Build a balanced portfolio

Many successful investors end up holding both residential and commercial assets. I don't see it as an either-or decision. Residential provides stability and growth. Commercial can provide higher income once the residential foundation is in place.

The key is timing and sequencing. Building a solid residential base first usually makes stepping into commercial more comfortable and less risky. It gives you equity, borrowing capacity and cash-flow resilience. Particularly for investors approaching retirement, a balanced approach can provide both income security and long-term financial flexibility.

Help the next generation earlier

Another conversation that comes up with people over 60 is helping their kids get into property.

Housing affordability has changed dramatically compared with when many baby boomers bought their first homes. Higher prices and deposits mean younger people often struggle to break in.

Providing financial assistance to the next generation while you're still alive can make a huge difference. It doesn't necessarily compromise your own security if done sensibly and it can strengthen family wealth across generations. You'll also have the pleasure of seeing the benefits firsthand.

Diversification still matters

One question that comes up a lot, particularly with people moving into their sixties and thinking about stability, income and risk, is whether they should change their investing focus from property to shares.

I'm not anti-shares at all. They absolutely have their place, especially from a diversification point of view. But for Australians heading into retirement, property still offers a combination of stability, income potential and long-term growth that's hard to ignore.

Over the past decade in particular, Australian property markets have shown themselves to be highly resilient. Through economic uncertainty, interest rate cycles and global disruptions, well-located residential property has generally held its value and continued to grow. That steady compounding effect is something retirees often find reassuring, especially compared to what can be sharp share market rises and falls.

Take Sydney. Over the past 10 years, house prices have close to doubled, which works out to around 7 per cent annual growth, depending on the suburb and property type. On top of that, rental income increases have been in the 3 to 5 per cent range. Capital growth and rental yields like these can be compelling for long-term investors.

Shares, of course, can also deliver strong returns. The Australian share market has averaged solid performance over the same period, especially when dividends are included. But the experience for investors can feel very different. Share market volatility can definitely be stressful.

Property generally moves more slowly. Prices don't fluctuate daily, which can make the investment feel more stable. That doesn't mean property prices never fall, but historically in Australia downturns have tended to be shorter and less severe than equity market corrections.

You only have to look at major events like the Global Financial Crisis or the COVID-19 pandemic period to see the difference. Share markets reacted quickly and sharply. Property markets softened in some areas but were largely supported by underlying housing demand, population growth and supply constraints. In many cases, values recovered relatively quickly and continued their long-term upward trend, which was generally true of the share market too.

For investors over 60, resilience can be particularly important. Since you're not usually looking to recover from major market shocks over a 30-year horizon, stability and predictable income become much higher priorities.

Another factor that often gets overlooked when choosing where best to invest is leverage. Property allows borrowing against assets in ways shares normally don't and that leverage can accelerate wealth creation over time, particularly when combined with rental income and long-term capital growth. Many Australians have built significant retirement wealth simply by holding property for decades, while tenants effectively help pay down the debt.

Structural factors that continue to support ongoing demand in Australian property markets are population growth, limited housing supply in desirable areas, planning restrictions and a strong cultural appetite for property ownership. Even as interest rates fluctuate, those underlying drivers remain.

Tax settings play a role too. Negative gearing, capital-gains-tax concessions for long-term holders and various methods of structuring property ownership can all benefit long-term investors.

Looking ahead, many analysts expect continued housing demand, combined with constrained supply, to support property values over the medium term. Interest rate movements will always influence the market, and there are moves to change negative gearing rules and/or reduce the capital-gains-tax discount, but the fundamentals remain reasonably strong.

None of this means shares should be ignored. They can offer liquidity, diversification and income through dividends. But for many Australians approaching or entering retirement, property often remains the backbone of their wealth simply because it combines growth, income and relative stability.

Which brings us back to the question: if you decide property is to be your focus, should that be residential, commercial or a mix (table 10.1)? It's not about choosing one over the other. It's about understanding how each fits into your overall strategy.

Table 10.1 ***comparing residential and commercial investment properties***

Investment type	Approx. 10-year annualised return (%)
Sydney house price growth (capital only)	~7
Sydney property total return (inc. rent)	~9–11+ (location-dependent)

Source: SQM Research

The role of financial advice

Before I go into detail, let me be clear: I'm not a financial adviser. What I can share with you comes from experience working in property and helping investors over many years. Clients, particularly those approaching retirement, often ask about financial advisers, because they want to make sure they've structured things properly.

Financial advice isn't a case of one-size-fits-all. There are advisers out there I trust and to whom I refer clients, but there isn't one

I'd recommend to everyone. It comes down to choosing one whose approach aligns with what you're trying to achieve.

Things have improved since the 2018 Royal Commission exposed some pretty questionable practices around commissions and conflicted advice. The financial services industry has cleaned itself up since then, but you should do your homework. You want someone who will act in your best interests and not someone pushing a particular investment type.

One issue I sometimes encounter is advisers who are strongly anti-property and advise clients to focus purely on shares. In my view, both have their place. I've had clients who prefer shares, managed funds or other investments. The important thing is that the advice you receive matches your goals, comfort level and lifestyle, and not the adviser's personal bias.

For the most part, I've been my own financial adviser. I built my portfolio, structured my investments and made decisions based on education, experience and professional input from accountants when needed. That approach worked for me, but I also recognise that not everyone wants to take that path.

Interestingly, I have begun working with a financial adviser recently, not because I suddenly need someone to tell me where to invest but because my situation has become more complex. With multiple properties, business interests, company structures and tax considerations to take into account, another layer of professional input around efficient structuring is useful.

The kind of structuring advice likely to be most useful for people over 60 might involve reviewing superannuation strategies, tax efficiency, estate planning, ownership structures or strategies for transitioning into retirement income streams. These issues are complicated and good advice can help avoid costly mistakes.

I always tell people that even when you're confident managing your own investments, it still makes sense to run structural questions past an accountant or licensed adviser. Should a property sit in your own name, in a trust or in super? Are you optimising tax outcomes? Are you set up properly for succession planning? Expert input can answer questions like these.

What I don't recommend is relying on casual advice from social media, forums or friends who mean well but don't have an in-depth knowledge of the field or of your financial situation. I see people who may, for instance, have inherited money or are going through a divorce or are approaching retirement or are sitting on significant cash reserves, asking strangers online what to do. That's very risky given the long-term consequences of such decisions.

There absolutely is a place for professional advice, whether it's from a financial planner, accountant, buyer's agent or other property specialist. The key is to make sure whoever you speak to understands your goals and respects the strategy with which you're comfortable.

Structure matters more than you might think

How you own property can make a surprisingly big difference, particularly once you move into your fifties and sixties. Most young investors buy property in their own name and don't think too much about structure. That's completely understandable because they're focused on getting into the market, building equity and growing their asset base.

But as retirement approaches it's no longer just about growth. It's also about income, tax efficiency, asset protection and what you will do with those assets down the track.

Depending on your income, holding property in your own name can sometimes mean paying higher marginal tax rates on rental income or capital gains, which is where alternative structures enter into the discussion.

Trusts are an option some investors consider as their portfolios grow. A trust can provide flexibility in how income is distributed which may help with tax efficiency across family members. It can also offer a level of asset protection in certain circumstances. That said, trusts come with additional costs, administration fees and compliance requirements, so again they're not for everyone. Like most things in property investing, the benefit depends on the individual situation.

Then there's property held within superannuation, particularly through self-managed super funds. That can be appealing for retirees looking to maximise income efficiency but, as discussed in chapter 9, SMSF property ownership isn't something to jump into without careful consideration.

One of the main reasons structure becomes more important later in life is estate planning. As people move closer to retirement, they start thinking more about how they'll pass assets on to the next generation. How property is owned will influence tax implications as well as flexibility around asset distribution.

It also affects income planning. If you're relying on rental income to support your retirement, the tax treatment of that income matters. Whether you hold a property personally or inside an SMSF, for example, can significantly affect how much of that income you actually get to keep.

Another factor is risk management. As portfolios grow, protecting assets becomes more important. Ownership structure can play a role in managing financial risk, legal exposure and long-term financial security.

The key point here is that no one structure is better than another across the board and further, because things don't stay the same, it's sensible to review how your properties are held from time to time. Life changes. Tax rules evolve. Financial goals shift. A structure that worked 10 years ago might still be perfectly fine, or it might benefit from adjustment.

Case study

Downsizing to create debt-free passive income

When Ninab and Riya came to talk with me, Ninab was 66 and had retired six months earlier and Riya was 59 and had not worked for around five years due to ongoing health issues. They had no further borrowing capacity, so any strategy needed to focus on maximising what they already owned rather than leveraging into new debt.

They were asset-rich and income-light. Their situation looked strong on paper, but they wanted advice on how to use their assets to achieve sustainable retirement income.

Their position at the time:

- a mortgage-free Sydney family home worth approximately $4.5 million
- an investment property in Melbourne worth around $1.5 million with a $700 000 mortgage

- three adult financially independent children
- virtually no superannuation.

The lack of super was largely due to Ninab running his plumbing business as a sole trader for decades without contributing to super. Riya had worked intermittently as a nurse but had taken significant time off, first to raise their children and later to deal with health challenges.

Around this time Ninab's father died, leaving them an inheritance of approximately $1.8 million. That inheritance created both opportunity and uncertainty. They wanted to use it wisely but weren't sure what the best approach would be.

What they wanted

Their goals were relatively straightforward and clear. They wanted financial security in retirement without having to worry about market volatility or relying on complicated financial products.

This required:

- reliable passive income
- debt reduction and financial simplicity
- assets they could pass on to their children
- a lifestyle property that required less maintenance than their Sydney home.

Property made sense to them because they understood it and had already used it to build wealth.

The strategy

Because they were empty nesters with a high-value, debt-free home the biggest opportunity lay in unlocking their equity.

(continued)

I suggested downsizing to free up capital, reduce maintenance responsibilities and create the cash needed to build a strong passive income base.

The initial plan was to:

- sell their Sydney home for around $4.5 million
- purchase a duplex-style downsizer for around $2 million
- avoid strata where possible to reduce ongoing costs
- use surplus cash plus inheritance to buy investment properties outright.

There is no capital gains tax payable on a primary residence, so selling their home would release tax-free equity.

This strategy would convert dormant equity into income-producing assets without introducing debt.

The result

The numbers were even better than expected. Their Sydney home sold for $4.75 million, well above initial estimates. They secured a high-quality duplex property for $2.2 million, which suited their downsizing goals perfectly.

The transaction costs were:

- stamp duty on the new home: approximately $103 000
- selling agent, marketing and legal costs: approximately $85 000.

After completing the sale, purchasing their new home and covering all associated costs, they were left with $2 382 000 in cash. With the $1.8 million inheritance, their total available funds for investment reached $4 182 000 in cash.

That gave them the flexibility they needed to build their freedom fund.

Building the freedom fund

Rather than chasing yield in volatile assets or complex financial structures, they decided to buy investment-grade property outright.

The objective was simple:

- 100 per cent positive cash flow
- Zero investment debt
- Long-term blue-chip growth
- Reliable income for retirement.

They purchased two high-quality properties:

Manly West, Brisbane

- *Purchase price:* $1 550 000
- *Stamp duty:* approximately $76 000
- *Property type:* Four-bedroom standalone home
- *Rental income:* $950 a week

Brighton, Melbourne (Bayside)

- *Purchase price:* $1.7 million
- *Stamp duty:* approximately $97 000
- *Property type:* Architecturally designed duplex-style property
- *Rental income:* $1120 a week

(continued)

Together, these properties generated $2070 a week in immediate passive income that was entirely unencumbered.

Final debt clean-up

They still owned their original Melbourne investment property which had a remaining mortgage of approximately $700 000. With their remaining cash reserves, they chose to eliminate that debt. After paying out this mortgage, they were left with approximately $50 000 in cash while holding three fully debt-free investment properties producing strong rental income.

Their financial position was transformed:

- No home loan
- No investment loans
- Significant weekly passive income
- High-quality assets in strong-growth locations

The outcome

Ninab and Riya effectively converted dormant home equity and inheritance funds into a retirement income engine.

They now have:

- a downsized, low-maintenance home
- three unencumbered investment properties
- around $3220 per week in rental income
- no debt exposure
- assets positioned in blue-chip growth markets.

I referred them to a financial planner as was my fiduciary duty, they chose to focus on property because they saw it as tangible, understandable and aligned with their comfort level.

They moved from asset-rich uncertainty to stable, debt-free retirement income.

I keep in touch with them. They're relaxed, financially secure and enjoying retirement without the stress of uncertainty.

Lifestyle comes first

What isn't talked about enough when people discuss property and retirement is that at a certain point it stops being purely a numbers exercise. It's not just about whether a suburb is going to outperform over the next 10 years. It's about whether you feel comfortable there, whether you're close to family, whether healthcare is accessible, whether the community suits your lifestyle. These things can have a huge impact on day-to-day happiness.

I see people who stay in their large family home because they've always lived there, although the property no longer suits them. The kids have moved out, maintenance is more onerous and the location might not work as well for them as it once did. That doesn't necessarily mean they should sell, but it's worth asking whether or not the property still supports their lifestyle.

Community connections become increasingly important. Being close to friends, family, services and social networks often contribute more to quality of life than squeezing out an extra percentage point of investment return.

Travel can be a real consideration too. Many retirees want the flexibility to spend time away from home, whether interstate, overseas or on extended trips. Owning a property that requires constant upkeep can be limiting, and downsizing, relocating or restructuring can create options.

I always say the ideal property strategy in retirement should support your lifestyle rather than dictate it. Financial optimisation still matters, of course, but it shouldn't come at the cost of comfort, health or enjoyment. Retirement is meant to be a time when the assets you've built start working for you, not the other way around.

When property decisions align with lifestyle goals, people generally feel more secure and more relaxed about their finances. And peace of mind is often just as valuable as financial returns.

Doing nothing may sometimes be the best move

There's often a lot of pressure around retirement to make big changes. Sell the house, restructure investments, move locations, try new strategies. Sometimes those changes make perfect sense. But not always.

If you love your home and it's paid off, your superannuation is healthy, income streams are stable, and you're not feeling financial stress, then maintaining your current set-up can be the right decision. There's no rule that says you must change things because you've hit a certain age.

In fact, I've seen people create unnecessary complexity by making changes they didn't really need to make. They chase new investments, restructure assets too aggressively or move properties when the existing arrangement was already working well. Stability has value, especially in retirement.

That said, doing nothing doesn't equate to ignoring your financial situation altogether. Regular reviews are still important. Circumstances evolve. Health considerations change. Family situations shift. Economic conditions move around. What works today might still work in five years, but it's worth checking.

Sometimes a review simply confirms that everything is on track. Sometimes it highlights small adjustments to improve income, reduce risk or enhance flexibility. Those tweaks don't have to be dramatic to be effective.

I often tell clients that a retirement property strategy is less about constant activity and more about thoughtful oversight. It's about making sure the assets you've built continue to support your goals, rather than allowing you to drift off course.

And for many Australians over 60, that reassurance alone makes a big difference. Knowing your plan is still working, your income is stable and your property position remains sound can remove a lot of background financial stress.

At the end of the day, property investing is less a race than a journey. Sometimes the smartest move is to stay the course, enjoy the lifestyle you've worked hard to build and let your assets continue to quietly do their job.

It's never too late to optimise

One of the most encouraging things I tell clients over 60 is that it's not too late to make small adjustments to improve their financial situation. Downsizing, restructuring investments, improving diversification or simply reviewing your plan can increase income, reduce stress and improve flexibility. Such adjustments can make a real difference.

Property has been central to wealth creation in Australia for decades, and it continues to play a major role in retirement planning. Used strategically, it can provide income, stability and lifestyle flexibility well into later life. Ultimately, retirement isn't about how many properties you own or how impressive your asset base looks. It's about how comfortably you live and how effectively your assets support the life you want.

Once that shift from accumulation to income happens, everything tends to fall into place. And that's really what retirement planning should be about.

One of the biggest rewards of a well-executed property investment career is the opportunity to leave a legacy, both for your family and loved ones and for those in need and causes you believe in, and this is the subject of the final chapter.

Key takeaways

- Downsizing is about unlocking equity and is one of the simplest and most effective financial adjustments you can make in later life.
- A successful portfolio for a retiree is one in which quality properties in diversified economies are the foundation.
- Property can help hedge against inflation because both rents and property values tend to rise over time.
- There are ways to get higher yields without taking big risks. Look for solid fundamentals: good locations, diverse economic drivers and strong tenant demand.
- Residential markets are influenced by population growth, housing supply, infrastructure and lifestyle factors. Commercial property is tied to business conditions, industry trends and economic cycles.
- Once you reach retirement it isn't about how many properties you own; it's about how effectively your assets support the life you want.

Chapter 11

What kind of legacy do you want to leave?

This chapter discusses creating ongoing generational wealth with a focus on paying forward that wealth in order to leave the world a better place.

For me, it's not only about how much money Renee and I need or even about setting our kids up for life, although those factors remain central. I'll continue to create and foster generational wealth, but I also want to help others who are less fortunate than we are.

I don't think of my legacy as just about giving people stuff. To begin with our two boys, it's not just about setting them up with a whole heap of properties down the track. There's a lot of knowledge I can share with them around the generation of material wealth, but they also need to understand the importance of support in the forms of sharing time and know-how. In other words, I want to educate them so they understand *how we got what we've got* so they can build on that and maybe one day teach their own kids how to continue that legacy.

Another aspect of legacy that's important to me is publishing this and other books about wealth creation. And then there's my music—something that's been a passion for me all my life. I'll come back to this.

Lloyd's core guiding principles

- I believe in paying it forward, once you're in a position to do so, so your kids have a better chance of attaining *their* dream lifestyles.
- I believe it's important to do what you love and love what you do.
- I believe in family and work–life balance.
- I believe in giving back.

Investment strategies for setting up the next generation

In our case, setting the kids up for life includes buying them a unit—a place they can live while they're young so they're not paying off someone else's mortgage. Later on they'll be able to rent it out to bring in cash flow.

Our sons are still very young—by the time this book comes out, my oldest will be only seven or eight. Of course we want them to follow their dreams, but Renee in particular would really struggle if they were to move overseas when they leave home. It would be nice if they were able to live close to us and when *they* have kids we'll have grandkids living near us too. So yeah, that's the hope, and as I'll explain, I'm doing what I can to make it a reality!

If we're still in Sydney, where property's pricey even by world standards, then realistically we will need to help our kids. As we've pointed out, it's very difficult for young people to raise the deposit for a place in Sydney or, for that matter, any Australian capital.

I've got a couple of properties in Sydney earmarked as part of our boys' inheritance. And two apartments I've bought in Sydney and Brisbane are strategically located should our kids choose to study at either the University of Sydney or the University of Queensland.

These are some of the ways I've thought ahead since quite early in the process of putting together a property portfolio. It's part of our strategy—but only part of it. Yours may need to be different.

The investment strategies I've laid out in *Set for Life* are different from those I advised in my first couple of books. The focus in *Positively Geared* and *Buy Now* was personal and family wealth-creation strategies. Here my focus is strategies that create *generational* wealth.

Strategy 1: Think ahead to create generational wealth

You need to fold your kids' futures into your own wealth-creation strategy—especially if you live in a capital city or a go-ahead regional area.

People who worry that it's going to get harder and harder to buy into property may well be right. But as this book shows, once you secure that first property—if you buy smart—it's a different story. The ever-growing price of Australian property means yours will almost certainly see substantial capital growth over time, as well as producing some cash flow while it appreciates.

That said, it *is* difficult for young people to get a foothold on that ladder, especially in our cities, and Australian property certainly won't be cheaper once our kids grow up and want to buy in. It will make things much easier for them if your property strategy sets them up as well.

Personal and generational wealth creation don't have to be mutually exclusive. With a few tweaks to your plan, you can add properties to your portfolio that will perform well for you *and* for your kids.

Strategy 2: Keep an eye out for suitable properties in your home town

To return to encouraging your kids and grandkids to live nearby down the track, when the time is right, you could do worse than buying something *in your area* that they can live in later on. This is not my usual advice on searching for investment properties but if you want to keep your kids close once they leave home, this might be a strategy!

If you call any Australian capital city home, you'll want to get in soon. By the start of 2026, median dwelling prices across all capitals, and even in some regional areas, were sitting at around a million dollars. And going on past performance, and the latest forecasts, they don't look like losing value anytime soon.

Depending on your city's or region's stage in the market cycle, you might want to buy those generational wealth properties sooner rather than later, but if you can't afford to buy property for your kids right now, that's okay. Having this goal as part of your overall freedom fund strategy means you can take a bit of time searching for properties that tick all your boxes, then strike when the market and your finances together allow it. That is, unless you're happy to move to wherever your kids end up (not something Renee and I are keen to do).

Strategy 3: Buy a well-located apartment or two

My long-term wealth-creation strategies don't typically include buying apartments because their potential for capital growth is less than that of houses. But a well-located boutique apartment can not only achieve good growth over time but also have better yields than a house. You can get decent cash flow while your asset appreciates.

I have bought apartments for that very reason—one in Alexandria, a blue-chip location 5 kilometres from Sydney's CBD, and another in Newstead, close to Brisbane's CBD.

Both produce good cash flow and are increasing in value.

But for me, and my family, there's another big benefit. Should either or both my kids end up going to Sydney Uni or UNSW, for example, they could live in the Alexandria apartment while they study. It's a good area, close to both big unis as well as to workplaces and other amenities, and the public transport is good.

Newstead is another good suburb, near the Brisbane CBD and with good access to UQ, Griffith and QUT and to potential workplaces. It would make a good base for either or both the kids should they move to Brisbane.

So sometimes it's okay to buy an apartment—especially if it's to serve a dual purpose such as wealth generation and, potentially, a rent-free home base for your kids while they're studying and becoming established in their own right.

More strategies for creating generational wealth

Some of these strategies are geared to more established investors; others can form part of a start-from-scratch strategy.

- Use equity from your home to purchase an investment property that will become an asset for the kids.
- Invest in cash-flow-producing properties, such as those that can generate a dual income. These might be duplexes or houses with granny flats or with enough space to build them.
- 'Land bank' to sell at a profit later, usually without building. You can improve your profit by getting a development application (DA) for a dwelling on the land, or CDC approval. I have gone into detail on these strategies in *Positively Geared*.
- Build duplexes so you can gain equity through subdivision that you can then use to pay off other debt faster. Build and sell both or keep one and sell the other to pay down or pay off other debt. See *Positively Geared*.
- Invest in property suitable for letting out through short-term stay sites or local real estate agents. This strategy can bring you a decent cash flow, and if the property is in the right area it will probably also get good capital growth over time. We let out our Mollymook holiday home via AirBnB for a while, and while it involved some work, it helped us pay off the mortgage faster.

Lloyd's strategy

Have multiple sources of income

Whether or not you have kids, if you want to create a legacy you first need to set yourself up. And to do that effectively, you need multiple sources of income.

There are various income models. You probably have your income-earning job. I did when I started out, though now I have my own business, my property portfolio and my books. They're all different sources of income but they'll all play a part of my legacy.

When I was a teacher, my side hustle was investing in property. Everything else stemmed from there.

I've learned that even if you don't have family wealth and you're starting from a low base, you can devise a strategy that forms the basis for creating generational wealth. But to really fast-track things and ensure you meet both your legacy goals and your dream lifestyle, it helps to have different sources of income.

If you're fortunate and have done your homework, your side hustle may turn into a full-time business as mine did, which comes with all sorts of benefits for generating wealth. And it becomes part of your legacy in its own right.

Create a business legacy

I started my own award-winning buyer's agency in 2014 when I resigned from teaching. This not only gave me an income stream, but allowed me to follow a career I'm passionate about. Renee, who gave me the idea for the business in the first place, now works in the agency one, two or two-and-a-half days a week—as much or as little as works for her.

I love what I've been able to create and am continuing to build, and a big thing for me is to pay that forward. One of the ways I can do that is to help our boys set up and run their own businesses when the time comes, should that be their passion.

Of course, if one or both the boys really want to work in our business, I'll facilitate that. But there will be no pressure on them to come into the business or to work in property or finance, or become buyer's agents—unless they're drawn to it. I'll help them understand my passion, then they can make their own choices.

I'll show them the fundamentals of running a business, using Aus Property Professionals as an example. I'll tell them what worked well but I won't leave out the mistakes I made during the start-up days so they can avoid making the same ones.

I'll teach them the importance of not thinking about the money when starting a business because I know from experience that if you're looking to help people and you look after other people first, then money and all that good stuff will follow.

Business success is of course partly about money, but that's not what keeps you going and what makes you happy every day. The real joy, the real satisfaction is in doing something you're passionate about and helping others while you're at it.

I never want my kids—or you—to lose sight of that.

Set yourself up for business success by doing what you love

But how do you actually get to the point at which you have both a successful business and other income streams? My tip for starting a business that works for you is to try to find a hole in the market, a service that not a lot of people are offering. If you can find a niche you want to fill, then you can really help people.

For example, when I started my business there weren't as many buyer's agents around as there are now, and most focused on standard investment properties. My niche was always about *manufacturing equity* and I was the only buyer's agent doing duplexes and then adding value through other strategies such as renovations.

My advice is, once you're in a position to be able to quit your day job, figure out how you can use your particular area of expertise or passion to provide something that adds value for people and that no-one else is doing yet. It's about spotting the gap. If you have the necessary expertise, you can really help people by offering something no-one else is.

Lloyd's business pathway: become a buyer's agent

I had no ambition to be a buyer's agent when I worked as a teacher, let alone to build my own buyer's agency. It was not part of the plan.

As it happened, the inspiration for my business—helping people use property to create financial freedom—came from my teaching music to kids with wealthy parents. I wanted to try to set myself up and later to set up my family, my kids. And I wanted to make a positive difference not just to my family's lives but to other people's lives.

I used to talk a lot about property at home, and eventually Renee said, 'You should write a blog about property so I don't have to listen to you talk about it all the time!' So I began writing a blog called Aus Property Powwow.

That was my initial 'business' name before I launched Aus Property Professionals. I didn't have any SEO on my blog posts, so I probably wasn't getting too many readers, but a few people got in touch and it got some exposure in the media. I was on 2GB radio at one stage, and in *Australian Property Investor* (API) magazine as an investor who'd had some success. And more people started to contact me seeking help with property investing. And that's how things started.

People were interested in what I'd done. They wanted to know, for example, how I'd gone about building a duplex and could I help them do that. At the time I didn't have any property qualifications or a licence so I was giving free but unofficial advice. I couldn't give specialist advice but I could offer a helping hand, some suggestions: they might consider doing this or that. I really enjoyed helping people. I loved meeting people in cafés to chat about property.

Renee said, 'You should try to get something going and help people officially.' That's when I enrolled in a Diploma in Property, which allowed me to become licensed, and I got a few other qualifications too.

You can take up to three years to complete the diploma, but I was done in three months because I worked on it online at night. Then I'd get up at 6 am to go to work. I'd start teaching at 7 am and knock off at 4 pm. I studied till about 3 am, sometimes getting only two or three hours' sleep a night for three months at a stretch. I was bashing my way through the assignments so I could start the business as a licensed and qualified buyer's agent. Fast-forward to today and I am now a licensed buyer's agent in most states in Australia, and Aus Property Professionals holds a corporate licence in most states as well.

Start a successful side hustle: passion, research and a market niche

If you want to reach your goal of financial freedom *and* create a legacy, it will be more difficult if a PAYG job is your principal income stream, even after you get onto the property ladder. If you can, find a side hustle, preferably something you feel you can do better than anyone else.

It's always good to follow your passion, but having a cool business idea is not enough. Ask yourself, is there a *need* for what I'm offering. Is the market already saturated or is there a particular gap you can fill?

My niche was always *manufacturing value* in ways that meant investors didn't have to wait 10 years for their property to increase in value. And no other buyer's agents were doing duplexes at the time so I made them my niche.

Once you've determined there is demand and a gap in the market, you'll need to research your target market. And if, for example, you're offering a service that involves dealing with people, things will work better if you like people! Play to your strengths.

My business philosophy: help people first, put money second

I began my business primarily because I wanted to help people who wanted to emulate what I'd done. That was my focus. What I didn't realise was just how much of an impact the business would have. People write to thank me for the help I've given them. They might have bought a property on my advice that's gone up in value by a couple of hundred thousand dollars over a couple of years. It's got them out of financial trouble and now they've got a strategy for acquiring the next property. Stories like this make me feel really good about what I do.

Beyond school: a real-world financial education

This book has explained how to set yourself up for life, and in this chapter we've begun to think about creating a legacy—paying it forward and giving back. Part of that legacy is knowledge.

In *Positively Geared* and *Buy Now,* I talk about the drive to get good marks in your school certificate or HSC in order to get a place at your preferred uni and to get a good degree, which will lead to a good job—and then working your whole life. What you're *not* typically taught is how to look after your finances. You're not taught that most people won't become wealthy by saving from their earnings.

What you need to *learn* is how to invest what money you earn to create more money in order to build wealth. So part of my legacy is the know-how I've gained over the years about all that—know-how I pass to my clients, my readers and my kids.

Help your kids get a start: encourage them to follow their passion

If our boys want to start businesses of their own down the track, of course we'll help them set that up. But of course they might want to start a company that has nothing to do with property or to get a job in finance. They both love martial arts so maybe they'll run a martial arts studio one day. Or perhaps they'll want to teach music, as I did, or become professional musicians. Whatever they choose, we'll be there to support them.

They'll get a big leg-up from the property and assets we'll be able to pass on to them as well as the knowledge (and contacts) to create a good financial setup and to know how to make smart decisions about their lives and goals. The knowledge we can share is part of our legacy too.

A legacy of knowledge

My goal with my books and podcast is to educate people, and I know that those books are helping lots of other people, and *their* families, to set themselves up for life. And if the royalties from my books outlast me, they will form part of a material legacy too.

My reason for writing these books wasn't to sell my services; I was happy with the number of clients who came to us. It was more because I thought I had a story to tell and I should get it out there. And I was reaching a different, wider audience.

In my first book I related how I came to be in the position of being able to retire from teaching at age 40 and enter a new profession and create wealth through property.

At the time I didn't really think anyone would want to read it but I thought I'd give it a go anyway. I talked about my strategies and illustrated them with case studies of investments and developments—mine but also those of some of our clients. I wanted to let people see how they could achieve financial freedom for themselves and their families by investing in property.

To my surprise, that first book has been the bestselling property-investment book in Australia for the past 10 years and the second bestselling Australian property-investment book of all time. So it's done very well. The money it would make wasn't front of mind while I was writing it. I was just hoping that a few readers might benefit from my sharing my experience and insights.

It was about getting information out there. I wanted to inform people about Australia's different property markets and how an understanding of how they work can make getting on the property ladder possible. I provided case studies on those various markets that asked questions such as: Why would I buy on the NSW Central Coast? Or on the Sunshine Coast? What are the demographics there? What's the infrastructure like?

I wanted to take my know-how and *pay it forward*.

A book potentially has a long life. With luck, *Set for Life* will remain in print for a while and readers will be able to access copies just as they'll be able to access copies of *Positively Geared (PG)* and *Buy Now*. And I hope these books will continue to inspire and educate people with good, practical advice. I hope readers will use the know-how passed on through my books to achieve financial freedom, and that they will *pass on* some of that knowledge together with the wealth that knowledge has enabled them to achieve. Again, it's about paying it forward.

Our boys might be 12 or 13 before they're old enough to grasp the concepts in my books. But I think it would be educational for them to read this stuff, too.

A legacy of smart property investors

From the books and from my work, at least five clients that I know of have been inspired to become buyer's agents themselves. I take the liberty of thinking of them as part of my legacy.

Over the past five years, many other new buyer's agents have come onto the scene, and many of them have told me they have read *PG* and been inspired to have a go.

My books didn't just inspire people to become buyer's agents. They inspired individuals all over Australia to become more educated and passionate about buying property strategically. My hope is the books have shown, and continue to show, you don't have to be rich to get on the property ladder.

I want *Set for Life* to help and inspire people too.

Other platforms for paying it forward

These days my platforms have grown. As a recognised property expert I'm a regular contributor to the media. As well as my own *Positively Geared* podcast, I'm featured on platforms including *Smart Property Investor* (SPI) and *CEO Magazine*'s podcast, and I'm regularly interviewed on TV and radio.

The reach to potential readers across social platforms is huge with Facebook, LinkedIn, X, Instagram, TikTok and the like. And that's fantastic. Because it means we can share our know-how with millions *more* people, who can in turn make their own positive impacts.

The bigger picture: a legacy beyond money

As I signposted at the start of this chapter, building a truly valuable legacy is not just about ensuring your kids are secure financially. It's also about supporting them in less money-centric ways.

Renee and I are agreed this latter kind of support is more important, in the end, than all the material stuff. You can have heaps of money and property and fancy cars without being happy if you're not following your passion and helping others as well as yourself. This is something I try never to lose sight of.

My parents were there for me and I want to be there for my kids.

Renee and I met through music. I was conducting a band in which she was playing clarinet from the age of about 10, I played in eisteddfods in Orange, the town where I grew up, and in a number of other regional towns. When I was at school, my parents, who took an active part in every aspect of my upbringing, accompanied me to state and national competitions, and that kind of support has influenced the way I'm raising my own kids.

I've always worked to be there for my family. I'm busy, as most of us are, but I make sure I'm around for them and for Renee. It may require juggling but it's possible to make these things work. And it's worth it. Because your *material* legacy is one thing, but it's only part of the picture.

Legacy encompasses a range of ways in which we can have a long-lived positive impact, and that's why we need to examine what's truly valuable in life.

My family's legacy of music

I've been playing in the Sydney City Brass Band for a while now. It's Australia's premier brass band, having been the national champions for three of the last four years. In 2026 we performed at the British Open Brass Band Championships, the world's leading brass band competition, and we are only the third band from Australia to have been invited. I was able to facilitate this trip by becoming a major sponsor of the band, enabling the expensive trip to be affordable for the musicians involved.

Music runs in the family. My parents also met through music. My dad's parents were musicians, so he grew up singing; indeed he considered becoming a professional singer. Dad's mum had a career as a singing and piano teacher and a conductor. She was the first Australian outside of Sydney to pass the Licentiate of Trinity College London (LTCL), a highly regarded qualification in music performance.

My grandfather, who had started the business dad was running, played tuba in the town band and Dad's auntie, his mum's sister, sang in operas at Covent Garden.

My dad had a very good voice too. He was offered a scholarship to study overseas but was discouraged by his auntie. She had disliked the constant travel and living out of suitcases of a professional singer, and Dad decided it wasn't for him. Apart from six years of active service in World War II, he lived all his life in Orange. He had no regrets because he led a full life, with music as a hobby. He sang in the local male choir and local musicals; I think that's where he met Mum, whose family were music lovers.

My family's musical legacy is part of what I hope to pass on to our kids. Caelen really looks up to Riley. Riley is learning the piano and I enjoy helping him practice. Caelen will begin to learn a musical instrument as soon as he's old enough. And if they both end up loving music, as I do, that's also a form of generational wealth.

Give now — don't wait

If you can afford it and if they need it, don't make your children wait until you die before passing on some of their inheritance, if only to allow them to get into the property market themselves. Much as we try to educate our kids in the importance of financial planning and wealth creation, we all know it's increasingly difficult for a young person to save the money for a deposit on their first property. A leg-up is really important. Of course, it may not be possible but if you've got equity in property you own, or are in a position to give your kids a couple of hundred thousand dollars for a deposit, I recommend you do so.

As I've explained, this isn't an entirely unselfish act. Your kids will be more likely to stay close if you make it easy for them to do so.

Wealth, success and trolls

Australians frequently manifest tall poppy syndrome. We do like to put down people who are successful, but I believe we all need something to aspire to.

Sure, there are people who can afford to buy properties with cash; they've got very successful businesses and enviable lifestyles. And it's tempting to believe that these privileges were just handed to them. Maybe their parents and grandparents were wealthy. Maybe they've benefited from wealth generated over generations.

James Packer is the son of media mogul Kerry Packer, who in turn was the son of successful newspaper boss Frank Packer. That's generational wealth. But there are plenty of people who've created their own fortunes. British businessman and Virgin tycoon Richard Branson springs to mind.

My takeaway is that you need to recognise it's okay to have money and property and material stuff, no matter what the people who like to cut down tall poppies say. And while you're taking steps towards getting set for life, be happy for those who are successful—that could be you some day.

In the end, it's what you do with that wealth that counts, so use it for good.

Successful people pay it forward *and* give back

A lot of successful people give back. Now I'm in a solid position financially, and am well on the way to setting my kids up for life, I donate a lot of money to charities. I see it as money well spent. Much of it is also tax-deductible, so it's a win-win.

By planning ahead, I've positioned myself to be able to 'pay it forward' to our kids and to share with those in need.

Aus Property Professionals has allowed me to make significant donations to charity. When I was a PAYG income earner I could donate a little here or there. Nowadays I can proudly donate thousands of dollars.

The message, I guess, is that *you can help more if you have more to give.* So for me, being successful with property and with my business has given me the leverage, time and money to be able to help others less fortunate. It's a great position to be in, and a great feeling.

At Aus Property Professionals, we're focused on helping everyday Australians grow their wealth through smart property investments, but we also believe in using our platform to drive broader meaningful change.

To this end, we are honoured to play a small part in Kenya's Laboso Caring & Regenerative Society Foundation. Their impact spans scholarships, school fees, classroom builds, improved sanitation, and empowering young people, especially girls, to complete their education and create better futures. We donate directly, with no middle person and no admin fees. When they need something we send the money straight to them.

We are also in discussions to partner with Virgin Unite, an initiative of Sir Richard Branson. This great charitable organisation unites entrepreneurs and change-makers to tackle some of the world's toughest challenges, from ocean protection to healthcare, climate action and human rights.

If you've read *Positively Geared* or *Buy Now*, you'll know this isn't new for me—it's just finally becoming more real. These initiatives mark the beginning of something much bigger than us. And if you're supporting Aus Property Professionals in any way, you're helping to make all this possible. So thank you, truly, for being on the journey.

Philanthropy for the future: working with Sir Richard Branson

I spent a week with Sir Richard Branson this year at his home on Necker Island in the Caribbean. I went sailing with Sir Richard and ate with him every day. He even had me playing tennis!

I had been invited as a finalist in the *CEO Magazine* awards, and Virgin Unite is connected with that. So they looked into my business and I guess they liked what they saw, including a lot of the charity stuff that we do. And because they're also big on giving back, I made a positive connection with Richard Branson's business partners.

It was an inspirational experience because, as well as Sir Richard, I met some 25 very successful international CEOs and others.

We were there to discuss how business could advance the greater good and help countries in the developing world.

Giving in a way that pays it forward: from Kilimanjaro to Kenyan schools

One of my side projects is to provide children with access to educational services. Since climbing Mount Kilimanjaro a few years ago and spending some time in local communities, it has been my passion to assist those in Africa who are less fortunate than me and my family.

My role consists of paying for the education of some of the kids and building the school. This includes laying cement floors because the school will not be recognised legally by Kenya's Department of Education until these are in place and the kids have somewhere proper to sit. I'm about to buy additional desks because another new classroom has been completed. All this is giving kids opportunities that they'd otherwise not have.

One recent morning I woke up to this message: 'We can now smile. Thank you, Lloyd, for bringing St Barnabas Sofia Junior School to this great level.'

I was talking about this with Riley, my seven-year-old, and he suggested ways we might be able to provide toys to the students. He often asks, 'Can we take this to give to the homeless?' or 'Can we take this to the Salvos?' We're starting those conversations early. Giving back will be normal for my boys as they grow up.

Homelessness might seem like an adult topic, but kids naturally want to help others. It's so important to educate our children so they recognise how lucky we are, and that two of the most important human rights are a safe roof over your head and access to education.

A substantial part of my income and business revenue goes to Kenya, but I donate to other charities too. For example, I just raised money for Dare to Cure, a children's cancer charity. I had to walk on fire and glass and get cuddled by a python, but it was for a good cause!

You may not be able to save the world but by giving back what you can afford, you can make it a better place. And that's a legacy you—and your kids—can be proud of.

Key takeaways

- Legacy is about more than just passing on material wealth — property and assets. It's also about sharing knowledge, experience and values. It encompasses a range of ways in which we can have a positive impact on our family and others.
- Paying it forward is also about creating generational wealth with a focus on leaving the world a better place.
- To create a legacy, you first need to set *yourself* up. If you want to reach your goal of financial freedom *and* create a legacy, find a side hustle, preferably something you feel you can do better than anyone else, something you're passionate about.
- Personal and generational wealth creation aren't mutually exclusive. With a few tweaks to your plan, you can add properties to your portfolio that will perform well for you *and* for your kids.
- When giving back, you can help more if you have more to give. Being successful with property and with my business has given me the leverage, time and money to be able to help others.

Conclusion

If you've made it this far, you're already ahead of most investors. So stick to the basics, stay disciplined and set yourself up for long-term success. Remember, this isn't about perfection; it's about direction.

Property investing isn't about luck; it's about preparation, research and having the knowledge and the guts to make a move when the numbers stack up. Because when it's hot the market moves quickly, and the best opportunities go to those who are prepared and decisive.

Don't get stuck waiting for the perfect time to buy and don't overthink every move. The most important things are to get started, keep learning and be prepared to adjust your plan as you go. And there's no shame in asking for help. Experts, such as buyer's agents, mortgage brokers and accountants, can help you cut through the noise and make smarter decisions.

Keep your perfect day in mind. Let it guide your decisions. Enjoy the unexpected wins along the way and appreciate those moments when they arrive, but don't let short-term setbacks derail you from the bigger plan.

Wealth is built with discipline and patience. Every property in your portfolio should have a purpose. Whether you're just getting your foot on the property ladder, chasing growth or yield, setting up the next generation or looking to make the world a better place, make sure your next investment move fits your long-term strategy.

I hope you now feel less overwhelmed and more confident about where you're headed than before you read *Set for Life*, and that you have a clearer vision of your future, a practical roadmap for getting there and a strategy that starts where you are today rather than where you wish you were.

And thanks for reading. If you enjoyed *Set for Life*, check out *Positively Geared* and *Buy Now*. They're available at all good bookshops (and even some bad ones). Or jump onto our website, AusPropertyProfessionals.com.au, and say g'day. I'm here to help you invest smarter and create lasting financial freedom.

If you ever feel yourself drifting off course, come back to the fundamentals. Revisit your strategy. Re-read the chapters that resonated most for you. And if you need more help refining your roadmap, reach out. Let's have a conversation and make sure your plan is solid.

Your freedom fund starts with a single decision, and you've already made it.

Get in touch

If you'd like to get in touch with me or follow my work, you can find me at:

- **Aus Property Professionals**
  auspropertyprofessionals.com.au
- **Base Camp Property Club**
  facebook.com/groups/basecamppropertyclub
- **Instagram**
  @Lloydedge_buyersagent
- **Email**
  lloyd@auspropertyprofessionals.com.au
- **LinkedIn**
  linkedin.com/in/lloyd-edge-b417a399
- **YouTube**
  youtube.com/@auspropprofessionals

You can also listen to my top-rating *Positively Geared* podcast on Apple, Spotify or wherever you listen to your podcasts.

Lloyd Edge
Sydney
March 2026

Index

Printed and bound by CPI Group (UK) Ltd, Croydon, CR0 4YY
20/07/2026
14925137-0002